Praise for *Leading Outside the Lines*

"*Leading Outside the Lines* is a vibrant book with a compelling message vital to the success of 21st-century organizations— the message that informal human relationships, when effectively integrated with formal structures and systems, can powerfully propel people forward. It's a profoundly important idea that all contemporary leaders must attend to. This book is rich with real-life examples of organizational turnaround and culture change— some of the most unique and engaging I've ever read—from actual leaders who tried, failed, learned, and succeeded. Jon Katzenbach and Zia Khan do a masterful job of weaving together these intriguing case examples with practical applications and useful assessment tools. This is a book about doing great work, making people proud, getting people connected, and living a values-driven life. It's a book you need to savor.

—**Jim Kouzes, coauthor,** *The Leadership Challenge,* **and**
   Dean's Executive Professor of Leadership,
   Leavey School of Business, Santa Clara University

"*Leading Outside the Lines* is an incredible gift to leaders in all three sectors—public, private, and social—working to move beyond the old walls, build the new, flexible, fluid management systems, and develop leaders of the future determined to build the organization of the future. This management guidebook brings the best of formal and informal organizational theory and experience to leaders at every level, across the enterprise.

—**Frances Hesselbein, chairman and founding president,**
   Leader to Leader Institute, formerly the Peter F. Drucker
   Foundation for Nonprofit Management

"Katzenbach and Khan demonstrate that you don't have to choose between inspiring employees and getting amazing results—the best organizations do both. With novel perspectives, great stories, and practical advice they show leaders how to get the best of both in ways that can transform organizations. This book belongs in the hands of everyone who refuses to accept business as usual."

—Chip Conley, CEO, Joie de Vivre, and author, *Peak*

"Strategy and hierarchy drive how organizations operate, but so too do personal networks and intuitive judgments that define an equally powerful informal world within. Drawing on richly developed illustrations ranging from the Bushmen of southern Africa to eBay, the Marine Corps, and Starbucks, *Leading Outside the Lines* provides a compelling account of how leaders can best capitalize on the hidden drivers of organizational life."

—Michael Useem, professor of management, Wharton School,
    University of Pennsylvania, and author, *The Leadership Moment*

"The rate of change in our business, and the need to move information at high speed across organizations, necessitated an innovative look at organizational structures and management styles. The ideas in *Leading Outside the Lines* helped speed and successfully shape our major change implementations."

—Stan Glasgow, president and chief operation officer,
    Sony Electronics Inc.

leading
outside
the lines

**How to Mobilize the (in)Formal Organization,
Energize Your Team, and Get Better Results**

Jon R. Katzenbach | Zia Khan

JOSSEY-BASS
A Wiley Imprint
www.josseybass.com

Published by Jossey-Bass
A Wiley Imprint
989 Market Street, San Francisco, CA 94103-1741—www.josseybass.com

Jossey-Bass books and products are available through most bookstores. To contact Jossey-Bass
directly call our Customer Care Department within the U.S. at 800-956-7739, outside the U.S. at
317-572-3986, or fax 317-572-4002.

Jossey-Bass also publishes its books in a variety of electronic formats. Some content that appears in
print may not be available in electronic books.

Library of Congress Cataloging-in-Publication Data

Katzenbach, Jon R.
  Leading outside the lines : how to mobilize the informal organization, energize your team,
and get better results / Jon R. Katzenbach, Zia Khan.—1st ed.
      p. cm.
  Includes bibliographical references and index.
  ISBN 978-0-470-58902-1 (cloth)
  1. Employee motivation. 2. Leadership. 3. Corporate culture. I. Inayat-Khan, Zia. II. Title.
  HF5549.5.M63K373 2010
  658.4'092—dc22

                                                                    2010003888

Printed in the United States of America
FIRST EDITION
HB Printing   10 9 8 7 6 5 4 3 2 1

Jon: To Marvin Bower, whose memory never fades

Zia: To my parents for their steadfast love and support

Contents

Introduction

Like Talking to a Wall

Something strange was going on at the call center.

It was one of those large open rooms, filled with cubicles, each occupied by a service rep wearing a headset and answering customer calls. The scene seemed typical of such workplaces, except for one thing: A ten-foot-high wall, clad in purple fabric, cut straight through the center of the room, separating half of the service representatives from the other half.

We had been asked by our client, a senior executive at a health benefits provider, to look at this recently redesigned call center for best practices that could be applied in the company's other call center locations.

Throughout the morning, the air had been filled with the steady murmur of voices as the reps calmly handled callers' questions with dispatch and efficiency. Around eleven o'clock, however, the sound of the voice coming from the cubicle closest to us, where a rep named Gloria sat, took on a new tone. Gloria's responses grew hesitant, even a bit defensive. She would start to say something and then stop as if interrupted by the caller. At last she said, "Let me put you on hold for a moment. I need to ask a colleague about this. I will be right back."

Gloria punched the hold button, slipped off her headset, and walked to the purple wall. "Frank!" she yelled, her lips no more than six inches from the purple fabric. "Yo!" we heard a man's voice replying from the far side.

"I've got a caller with a question about COBRA payment for a laid-off worker's partner," Gloria called. "She wants to know if . . ." And Gloria went on with a detailed question. As soon as she was finished, Frank immediately called back the answer. "Got it," Gloria said, hurried back to her cubicle, clamped on her headset, and picked up the call. "So, here's the story," she said to the caller, and in a moment the matter was resolved.

At her next break, we asked Gloria about the wall. "It's ridiculous," she said. "When the customer service organization was reorganized about six months ago, the wall was put up. The idea was to separate us into distinct teams to improve focus and efficiency. But we often have to interact across teams and sometimes shouting through the wall is the quickest way to get an answer."

Over the course of three days of observation, we witnessed several more of these "through-the-wall" conversations. Later, when we brought up the issue of the wall with our client, he said it was news to him, even though he had been involved in the reorganization. Within a few weeks, the wall had been removed, the teams had been reintegrated, and the yelling had stopped.[1]

THE WALL AS AN ANALOGUE

It's rare to see a physical wall that is such a perfect analogue for an organizational wall. Most of the walls in companies of all kinds are intangible, invisible, and often unknown to senior management.

Although the call center wall seemed absurd, it had been erected for perfectly good and rational reasons that had to do with lines of business, reporting structures, and cost management. But the wall ended up getting in the way of real work that people had to do, so they found their own ways of getting around it.

To us, the wall represented the formal, hierarchical organization—the *lines,* if you will, that can be drawn to show the official relationships and power structures and workflows and channels of communication. The shouting through the wall represented the informal organization—the space, relationships, and behaviors that exist *outside* those formal lines.

It's tempting to see one or the other—the formal or informal approach—as the right or the wrong way. The call center representatives could certainly wonder what management had been thinking when they restructured the organization and put up the wall between the teams. Management could shake their heads when they heard about employees working across organizational lines and yelling through the wall.

In most companies, the formal organization is still seen as the right approach, the default structure. Especially if you have been trained in the hard disciplines (finance, technology, or operations management) as so many senior leaders have, you tend to work most naturally through tangibles like job descriptions, organization charts, process flows, scorecards, and physical structures. There is nothing wrong in that. However, you may be less comfortable dealing with the fuzzier aspects of an organization (informal networks, cultural norms, emotional realities, and peer pressure) even if you recognize their importance. Leading outside the lines is harder than managing within the formal lines, partly because that territory is less well defined, less studied, and less written about.

Even so, the formal and informal organizations invariably find some way to coexist. For years the informal typically prevailed mostly in small organizations or "skunk works," while in larger organizations the formal tended to prevail. This will not be true much longer. In the current business environment—characterized by a rapid rate of change, increasing globalization, and the rise of Web-based social networks—more and more companies are finding that the best way to create lasting value is by nurturing all kinds of informal and non-hierarchical initiatives rather than by relying so heavily on formal top-down rules of engagement.

To make a shift toward the informal is not easy. It is, however, an effort that is really worth making. Increasingly, those companies that can *mobilize* the informal organization as effectively as they *manage* the formal—that is, integrate the two and achieve a balance of complementary benefits—are the companies that can create a real and sustainable competitive advantage. "The best of both" is the name of the game now.

Specifically, these organizations are ahead of the curve because they successfully accomplish more than one balancing act:

- They foster, encourage, and support deep values that inform the decisions and actions taken at all levels of the formal structure. However, their values are also evident in the informal attitudes, interactions, and behaviors of people throughout the organization.
- They ensure that formal, long-range strategy is understood rationally by people working on the front lines of the operation. However, they also provide emotional and visceral support, so the strategy permeates all aspects of the work.
- They retain the efficiency and clarity of the well-defined structures that define the formal organization while also capitalizing on the flexibility and speed of the social networks and peer interactions that connect people informally.
- They ensure that in addition to the formal methods of compensation and reward, including pay, benefits, bonuses, and well-defined forms of recognition, employees have emotional sources of motivation that commit them in ways that the formal mechanisms cannot.

The Origins of This Book

We have come to understand the formal and informal organizations through decades of research, client work, and personal experience spanning industries, sectors, and nations.

Jon Katzenbach (generally known as Katz) has advised organizations for more than forty years, first at McKinsey & Company and then at his own firm, Katzenbach Partners (now part of Booz & Company). Katz has long been fascinated by team dynamics, how organizations function, and what motivates people and has written extensively about these topics in many articles and books, including his classic work, with Douglas Smith, *The Wisdom of Teams*.

Zia Khan joined the world of consulting after many years in academia. At Katzenbach Partners, he led several of the client engagements that led to the development of the ideas and methodologies described in this book. Zia's work focuses on the approaches and systems that drive strategy and improve organizational performance. He is currently vice president for strategy and evaluation at the Rockefeller Foundation.

So it has taken many years—and at least two epiphanies—for us to understand the ways of formal and informal organizations. Perhaps we were slow learners, but we sense we are not in a minority.

The first of the two epiphanies came over dinner one warm summer night in Montreal. That day we had engaged in a particularly interesting conversation with a senior vice president of strategy. His view was that the frontline workers in his company did not like the recent reorganization, and no matter how the formal structures were changed, kept right on acting and thinking as if the business were the same as it always had been.

Over dinner we talked about the issue of alignment at our client's company. Was that the problem? We decided that it was, but not in quite the way we normally think about it. In reorganizations like this one, our goal is usually to align the rational actions of management and employees of a new unit in support of the structural change. In this case, however, the alignment was among the managers of the old regionally focused organizational units that had been reorganized out of existence. These folks were communicating through an informal network to align their peers in very effective *resistance* to the change.

This alignment, we agreed, was deliberate. They had chosen not to communicate openly through the normal channels, such as staff or unit meetings, or documents or presentations, but rather through their informal networks. The communication was spontaneous and unrecorded and was devoted to denigrating the idea of the reorganization with the purpose of keeping the managers' power bases intact. Things were out of balance; the new formal organization was defined by customer segments, yet the informal organization remained regionally strongly aligned.

Our conclusion was that these informal regional networks, although more amorphous and less structured than the formal network, could nevertheless be identified and defined and managed, just as these resisters were doing. So if these managers could mobilize an informal network to resist change, why couldn't such mobilization become a standard managerial practice? Why couldn't formal managers make purposeful use of informal networks to achieve a goal or bring about a change?

The answer: they could. That was epiphany number one.

The second epiphany emerged a couple of years later. By that time, our thinking about the relation of the formal and informal organizations had progressed a good deal. We had become convinced of the power of the informal organization to help create both short- and long-term advantage. We spoke about the topic regularly with clients and at conferences. As the various social networking phenomena, such as Facebook and LinkedIn and Twitter, gained attention, journalists and other observers got intrigued by the subject, too. Often, they would seek our opinions on the relevance of social networking to business organizations. Social networking was the talk of the time.

Not everyone, however, was so enamored of the idea of the informal organization and the importance of social networking to business. At a CEO roundtable in Silicon Valley, we made some remarks about the formal-informal relationship and then asked for questions and comments. One CEO, who had become increasingly agitated during our presentation, jumped up. "The last thing I need is more informality," he barked. "I've worked very hard to establish a few commonsense, replicable processes—which I am sure you would describe as overly formal—that our company desperately needed, because we were losing share, losing money, and losing customers. Without those formal elements, I'm convinced that we would have gone under. But just when we were starting to operate with a little more order and discipline and things were starting to turn around, guess what happens? An engineer, who'd been with the company a long time, barges into my office—complete with beard and sandals, I might add—and tells me that my formal processes and uptight procedures are killing the soul of the company! That's what the informal organization is to me. Clueless about business realities."

That CEO was not alone in this view. Nor was this view wrong. We heard enough pushback from others at that event and at others that we did some soul-searching. Perhaps we had been overemphasizing the importance of the informal, and, in essence, throwing out the baby with the bathwater?

Those two epiphanies—first, that the informal could successfully be mobilized and second that the informal is not a complete solution—helped bring us to the understanding that managers must find ways to get the formal and informal working together. Most important, the optimal balance between the two will look very different depending on the company, the business, and the circumstances. Those insights also helped us see that organizations that learn how to mobilize their informal organizations while maintaining and reinforcing formal structures—be it Gentle Giant Moving Company, Southwest Airlines, Public School 130 in New York, or the Orpheus Chamber Orchestra—are uniquely powerful. They can improve their performance and sustain it over a long period of time.

As we've said, most of our learning has come from working closely with clients on real performance problems. Rather than theories, clients are interested in how our ideas and pragmatic approaches could help their people and their companies perform better. Time and time again in our client work we saw managers trying to realize a strategic intent only through formal means. The more frustrated they became, the harder they tugged at the formal levers. We helped them see that they also needed help from the informal organization to accomplish bigger goals.

Although we typically worked with our clients at the front end of an initiative to help define a vision and chart a course, we also worked with them in every area of the organization, both the formal and the informal. Watching the full cycle from vision to execution helped us understand the difference between ideas that lead to impact and ones that are management fads. By testing our ideas through real experiences, we were able to refine our ideas as we went along, and, most important, learn how to apply those ideas to drive organizational change and sustain performance improvements.

This client experience with gaining results through the right balance of the formal and informal is shared throughout this book. At the same time, we don't claim to have all the answers. Getting the best from both is a continuing challenge.

About the Content and Structure of the Book

Writers of books on organization tend to fall into one of two camps. Either they are formalists, who seek to bring better order to what they see as chaotic organizations, or they are informalists, who believe that organizations are too orderly and need more soul. In fact, the two groups are distinct enough in their views, and have been so for a long enough time, that they have had a variety of names attached to them. There is the "scientific management" school versus the "human relations" school; those who follow McGregor's Theory X and those who espouse Theory Y.[2] There have been many books written on both aspects of organization.

What has been missing, in our opinion, is a book that focuses on the informal organization but does so *with a realistic context that incorporates the formal and rational dimension of organization performance.* We are advocates and students of the informal, but we are also advocates and students of programmatic management, teachable methods, and quantifiable business impact.

So, in this book, we define as clearly as we can what the informal organization is. We also describe, with as much specificity as we can provide, how the informal can be mobilized and how it can be integrated with the formal elements of the company to achieve better performance.

In Part One, "Using the Informal to Enhance the Formal," we describe the two organizational dimensions, how the balance between them can shift, and how to integrate the two.

In Part Two, "Motivating Individual Performance," we explore the importance of the work itself and the role of values, and we discuss performance and how it must be the goal and the enabler for mobilization of the informal.

In Part Three, "Mobilizing Organizational Change," we talk about how to achieve strategic goals by setting free the "fast zebras" in the organization and melting the "frozen tundra" of middle management, and we discuss ways managers can mobilize the informal in transformational efforts.

Finally, we look at the relevance of the informal organization to a number of typical business initiatives (such as strategic planning and innovation) and how it affects different players, from individual contributors to senior leaders.

There are also two appendixes: a description of our research methodology and sources and a diagnostic tool.

●　●　●　●　●　●　●　●　●

When taking their organization in a new direction, leaders often start by working within the formal lines of the organization. They establish metrics and set goals, write plans, define rules of engagement, refine or create processes and programs, and tinker with hierarchies and structures.

Too often, these formal efforts don't get adequate traction as quickly as the leaders would like. As a result, the initiative takes far too long, goes awry, or stalls. Most major change efforts, in fact, peter out within two years of their inception. The few companies that make it past that barrier can achieve a sustainable performance advantage.

What's more, the informal aspects of the change—the ones that require action and leadership outside the lines—are usually harder for competitors to see. They are also harder to replicate than the formal elements (which are more easily copied as "best practices"), and that further sharpens the advantage.

Our goal with this book is to help leaders, particularly those who are already effective at leading within the lines, take a step back, look at the whole page, and see where and how they might also lead outside the lines most effectively and, as a result, have more impact. To do so does not require that they possess mystical talents or become expert in social networking. All it takes is an open mind, a willingness to adopt some new behaviors as necessary, a focus on execution, a strong desire to achieve real and long-lasting results—and an ability to see the vast performance potential that lies outside the lines.

PART ONE

USING THE INFORMAL TO ENHANCE THE FORMAL

The informal organization can create effects that seem like magic. They're amazing to watch, but it's difficult to know how to produce them. These intangible, often emotional aspects of the informal organization exist right alongside the more evident and rational aspects of the formal organization. The key is to understand that the informal delivers its greatest benefits when it is balanced with the formal. Maintaining a balance is harder to do than it may seem, as the balance point constantly shifts. However, by creating and sustaining a balance between the informal and formal elements, organizations can achieve the best of both in ways that provide significant advantages.

In Part One, we offer a quick history of the study of organizational behavior and discuss why an either/or mindset—rationalist or humanist—has usually prevailed. We explore several examples that stem from our personal experiences as well as illustrations from large and small business case studies. While business applications are our focus, we include two nonbusiness groups that illustrate the diversity and timeless origins of the issues—the Orpheus Chamber Orchestra in New York, and the !Kung tribes in Africa. By examining these two organizations, both of which are nonhierarchical and take very different approaches to leadership, we can get a richer understanding of the group dynamics that operate in all companies, business sectors, and cultures.

• • • • • • • • •

1

The Logic of the Formal; the Magic of the Informal

"Logic only gives man what he needs. . . . Magic gives him what he wants," author Tom Robbins once wrote.[1] The tension between the mind and the heart and the desire to integrate the two have been grist for the writer's mill for centuries. Management theorists, by contrast, have focused their efforts on one aspect of this tension or the other and have spent the past hundred years debating each other about which is more important. Our intention in this chapter is to show that it is not a question of either/or but rather of understanding what benefits the formal and informal offer, and why they need to work together.

The Head-Heart Debate: A Brief History

The rational school of management dominated business organizations for the first half of the twentieth century. Its roots are in the research of Frederick Taylor, often dubbed the father of scientific management.[2] Taylor stressed the need for using scientific rigor to select, train, and develop workers. He believed in cooperating with workers to ensure the success of his scientific methodology, dividing work nearly equally between managers and employees as a rational approach to optimizing performance.

Taylor's principles made sense. Prior to World War II, they were used in many factories, often with surprising improvements in productivity. Taylor advocated that all organizations could use what he called "time and motion studies" to improve efficiency and unlock hidden performance potential. Eventually, Taylor's ideas about scientific management spread from Henry Ford's automobile assembly lines all the way to the home.

Later, a different school of thought emerged that took a very different, much more emotional, approach to the practice of management. In 1960, Douglas McGregor published *The Human Side of Enterprise,* in which he identified two theories of individual work behavior.[3] Theory X assumed that people dislike work, prefer to be directed, and are motivated primarily by monetary rewards and punishments. This theory aligned with the rational approach to management. His second theory, Theory Y, assumed that people enjoy work, seek responsibility, and are motivated by purpose, feelings, and fulfillment.

Theory Y echoes the writings of other notable thinkers of the era. In 1954, Abraham Maslow placed self-actualization at the top of his hierarchy of needs.[4] In essence, this hierarchy refers to how people feel about who they are as individuals, what they do, and why they do it—and often, the people they do it with. Frederick Herzberg, in an almost desperately titled article, "One More Time: How Do You Motivate Employees?" answered his question by arguing that people are emotionally motivated by meeting challenges, taking responsibility, and doing work that they can feel good about performing well.[5]

Advocates of both the rational and emotional approaches have rarely sought to integrate their perspectives—in other words, to see if there was a possibility for "and" instead of "either/or."[6] Stanford professor Harold Leavitt, author of many books, including *Managerial*

Psychology and *Top Down,* from which the following passage is taken, describes how the two camps studying organizational performance in the 1950s viewed each other:

> One tiny skirmish of that great battle took place at MIT, where a handful of us were graduate students. We were proud and perhaps arrogant acolytes of McGregor, the pioneering humanizer of Theory Y fame. Our hot little group called itself "the people-people" and inhabited the third floor of MIT's Building 1. Our systemizing enemy—the hard-headed accounting, finance, and "principles of management" people, along with Taylor's progeny, the industrial engineers—held down the first floor of the same building.
>
> We people-people were sometimes required to take first-floor courses, all sorts of systemizing foolishness about such inhuman stuff as financial controls and cost-accounting. As you might guess, those forays into enemy territory served only to shore up our faith in our third floor's humanizing creed. And as our commitment to that creed grew, so did our scorn for the first floor's apostasy. Those first-floor guys were blind to Truth down there, intransigent, prejudiced, just plain wrong. They had adding machines where their hearts should have been. They didn't even comprehend our sacred words: *morale, motivation, participation.* We called the first-floor folks "make-a-buck Neanderthals." They called us "the happiness boys."[7]

While Leavitt's story may be a little tongue-in-cheek, it's not an exaggeration to say that similar battles still take place, and not just among academics but also among leaders at all levels of business organizations. There are serious disagreements about how best to get employees focused on what the leaders believe to be important to improve performance and achieve success in the enterprise.

We have watched and participated in many of these debates, in many companies, and with leaders who inhabit both camps—and a few who understood the importance of both. But our exposure to the head-heart debate goes back much further, to well before either of us got involved in management consulting.

How Katz Discovered the Informal

Katz graduated from Stanford University in 1954 with a degree in economics, making him, by training at least, a charter member of the formalist club. He spent his college days immersed in economic analysis, structured problem solving, and rational decision making.

The United States was still in the Korean War when Katz graduated. Had he waited to be drafted, Katz would have had no choice about which service he entered, so he decided to apply for the Navy's Officer Candidate School. He was accepted, graduated, then went on to the Navy's school for Supply Corps officers.

For a formalist like Katz, the military was fascinating. To this day, he follows developments in the procedures, programs, and rules of engagement that contribute to effective supply operations.

Katz got his first real assignment, as Disbursing and Assistant Supply Officer, aboard the amphibious ship USS *Whetstone*. His immediate superior, Lt. John Sandrock, had several years of experience in the Supply Corps and fit the stereotypical image of a good naval officer. He was tall, well-groomed, and commanding in every way. He maintained a well-defined arm's-length relationship with the members of his crew. He enforced rules and regulations to the letter and demanded that his men do the same.

After a year aboard the *Whetstone*, Katz was transferred to the USS *Nicholas*, then stationed in Pearl Harbor, where he served alongside Supply Officer Lt. Charlie Stewart. The *Nicholas* was a bit creaky and rusty, since it was then the oldest active escort destroyer in the Pacific fleet.

Charlie was Mr. Informal, or appeared to be, anyway, and this baffled Katz at first. Unlike Lt. Sandrock, Charlie's uniforms were, like the ship itself, worn and rumpled. Nor did his conversation suggest much interest in rules and regulations. But he had very close relationships with the sailors under his command. And he ran a remarkable supply operation. In fact, in Charlie's final year of duty on the *Nicholas,* the ship was awarded the Navy E Ribbon (E for efficiency) for having the best supply operation in the Pacific Fleet for its type of vessel.

The win was not accidental. Charlie and his crew had been working toward the coveted E for three years. The ship had the tidiest store, its disbursing records were flawless, and the storerooms and inventory were maintained as brilliantly as any Wal-Mart is today. Even the galley was known for the quality of its food and its speedy service. Not an easy trick aboard a creaky, rusty old ship at sea.

Although Katz didn't apply the term at the time, Charlie's operation clearly had an informal advantage. Yes, every sailor had the formal aspects of his job down pat. But that was not what distinguished the group—rather, it was the pride they took in their work and the emotional commitment they had to their jobs. "I wouldn't want to disappoint Charlie," they often said.

So effective was the supply group that Charlie's role in it seemed almost unnecessary. After all, the guys were almost entirely self-regulated. Charlie rarely made a suggestion, let alone gave an order. So Katz began to think he was the luckiest guy in the Supply Corps. When Charlie eventually moved on to his next ship and Katz took over the post, as was likely to happen, Katz figured that his job would be easy. He would just follow the rules and procedures already in place and keep things rolling as they had been. How hard could that be?

Of course, Katz had so completely focused on the formal elements of Charlie's organization that he had not really noticed the informal aspects that Charlie was so good at, thinking them incidental, even irrelevant.

Then came a revelatory moment. It happened during an admiral's inspection of the *Nicholas,* which was anchored in Pearl Harbor at the time. The day before the admiral was due to arrive, the captain of the *Nicholas* assembled his officers to review the procedure for receiving the admiral as he boarded ship. Two of the officers, however, could not attend the meeting. Charlie Stewart was on shore liberty and William Inskeep was on duty.

A key element of the formal reception of an admiral is a "sword salute" that requires that the receiving officers smartly, and in unison, withdraw their swords from their scabbards and snap the handles to the proper position against their chests. The captain particularly wanted to discuss the sword salute with his officers, because they had never actually worn or used their swords, nor had they ever been called upon to execute the salute. So the potential for serious harm existed.

Unfortunately, the two missing officers, Stewart and Inskeep, would be the "officers of the deck" on the day of the admiral's visit. That meant they would be the officers closest to the admiral as he came on board and the ones to initiate the sword salute.

The day arrived. Stewart and Inskeep took their places. The admiral stepped aboard. Inskeep grabbed the handle of his sword, clumsily yanked the blade out of the scabbard, and started to raise it into position. Charlie Stewart, at the same instant, sharply angled his arm upward and snapped his hand to his forehead in a crisp salute. Inskeep, his sword in motion, glanced at Charlie, wondering what was going on, and in that split second of wandering focus, the tip of his blade poked the brim of the admiral's cap. Everyone gasped as the cap flew off the admiral's head and went soaring into the ocean far below.

Charlie's informal organization had saved the day for him. It turned out that, during the meeting with his officers, the captain had concluded that the sword salute was too complicated and dangerous and had instructed his men to execute the standard hand salute instead. As soon as Charlie returned from his shore leave, his men informed him of the change so he was prepared when the admiral arrived. Inskeep, however, did not have the same kind of close relationship with his men and they had failed to give him a heads-up on the change in procedure. The "it's not my job, man" attitude prevailed.

The image of the admiral's hat slowly sinking to the bottom of the sea has become a compelling reminder for Katz that the informal takes care of its own when the formal does not.

It's interesting that Katz learned the importance of the informal while serving in the military—an organization that surpasses all others for its focus on hierarchy, formality, rules, and regulations. And yet what he came to realize is that the Navy (and other armed forces he has since studied) is so driven by emotion—trust, courage, fear, loyalty—that it could not function at all without an informal complement to its rigorous formal structure.

THE OVERLOOKED INFLUENCE OF EMOTIONS

If Katz had asked Lt. Sandrock—he of the well-pressed uniform and well-thumbed rulebook—if emotional commitment was important to his operation and if the feelings of his crewmen mattered, it is likely that Sandrock would have said, "Yes, but not nearly as much as process and execution."

Today, when we ask that question of managers and executives, especially in large companies, their answer tends to be about the same as Sandrock's would surely have been.

Formalists view the world through the lens of rationality—they value logic, analysis, data, and frameworks. They manage through formal processes and programs (usually devised and enforced by a select group of senior executives). These formal elements are promulgated through the organization in protocols and memos and enforced with comprehensive control-and-reward systems. If formalist managers accept that an emotional commitment is important, they tend to believe that it is a by-product of the right rational approach—employees will eventually see the logic of a good plan and will feel good about it.

These mechanisms rarely take emotional issues into account, but that does not mean that people don't react emotionally to them. They do—it's just that their reactions are often more negative than positive. As a result, they adopt attitudes and engage in behaviors counter to the plan and to what seems rational to the makers of the plan. Over and over again, we hear executives say that they just don't understand why their employees are not "on board." Didn't they get the memo?

However, rational clarity does not always create the emotional commitment that motivates a desired behavior. And when emotional factors are not taken into account, organizations fall short of their intended goals.

The fundamental issue is that formalist managers do not fully understand or believe in the importance and power of emotions in effecting change. They discount the degree to which human behavior is emotionally determined. They also see it as difficult, if not impossible, to manage or control emotional forces.

We do not want to diminish the value of rational structures and logical plans. At the same time, however, the bulk of our experience and research over the past several years has caused us to believe that emotional influences shape attitudes and drive behaviors as much as logical arguments and rational influences—and often have more impact.

THE LOGIC OF THE FORMAL

Why do managers favor the rational approach and rely on top-down execution efforts?

Largely because the mechanisms of the formal organization can be clearly defined, named, captured in written form, and measured. They include

- *Strategy.* A set of priorities, plans, and performance objectives that guide choices throughout the organization in how to best use resources and deploy capabilities.
- *Structures.* The lines and boxes that determine who reports to whom for what and that help align the decision making needed to achieve the organization's strategy.
- *Processes and procedures.* The written ground rules that determine the information and work flows needed to efficiently carry out the organization's day-to-day tasks.
- *Programs and initiatives.* Sets of goals, work plans, rules of engagement, and resources dedicated to achieving specific objectives within defined time lines.
- *Performance goals and metrics.* The explicit targets and measures that can be used to monitor and evaluate the performance of different groups and individuals.

Virtually all of these formal mechanisms can be found in official documents. In fact, the capture of these formal mechanisms in written form is crucial. It enables them to become fixed, made available for approval and subsequent reference, and easy to distribute to large numbers of people in precisely the same way every time. This is how the formal lines of organization become well known.

Unlike face-to-face meetings, conversations, social networks, and actions—which are more ephemeral—these formal documents bring precision and permanence. They officially document the outcomes of rational and analytical problem-solving processes. They carry a sense of authority. The organization chart, the role description, the scorecard—all can be referenced in ways that are especially useful in times of disagreement or disruption.

All of this is sensible and good. The formal comprises the nuts-and-bolts hardware that runs the machinery of business. Formal mechanisms provide time-tested templates that users of leadership systems can understand and follow and that can be passed along from one generation of leaders to the next. The formal organization helps create efficiency, clarify authority, communicate priorities, and align rationally driven behaviors around common objectives. Every company needs these logical things, so it's no wonder that most leaders rely so heavily on the formal—and therefore lead primarily within the lines.

RATIONALITY HAS ITS LIMITS

When formalist leaders want to make a change of some kind, however, their reliance on the formal organization may not serve them so well. They invariably overemphasize the rational case, especially when they want to make an unanticipated change of some kind, explaining in excruciating detail why the new plan is important. They will explore what competitors are doing, describe customer segmentations, go through elaborate financial forecasts, discuss corporate objectives at length, and explain scorecards in endless detail. Their assumption is that once the rest of the organization understands the logic of why certain behaviors are important, they will get it and do what's expected. If it's rational and explained properly, there shouldn't be a problem.

But there often is. For a workforce to be motivated to make a change in behavior, people need to believe that their individual and team efforts have a meaningful personal purpose that connects them emotionally to important priorities of their work situation. To that end, leaders need to be able to translate vision, targets, and strategies into personal purpose, accomplishments, and choices that each one of their people can understand and feel good about pursuing.

It's impossible to do this without drawing on strong emotional support. That's why formal methods frequently fail to elicit the level of performance that many leaders want. They are "rationally constrained." They simply don't allow room for the emotional determinants of behavior. These exist outside the lines of rational argument and the formal organization.

Any effort to create rational understanding has rapidly diminishing returns if it does not take into account that people's choices and behaviors are determined as much by emotional responses as by logical argument—and the former seldom follow the latter.

That's where the informal comes in.

THE MAGIC OF THE INFORMAL

The informal isn't as easily defined as the formal, because it does not have the clear structural boundaries that the formal has. Its elements often overlap and don't follow the clean principles of "mutually exclusive, comprehensively exhaustive" that analytical thinkers prefer. In essence, the informal is the aggregate of organizational elements that primarily influence behavior through emotional means.

And, unlike the formal elements, the informal elements of an organization rarely appear as written instructions. Even so, they can still be identified and named. They include

- *Shared values.* These are the shared beliefs and norms for taking action and making decisions as demonstrated individually and collectively. These often differ from the values that are formally stated and displayed. For example, some organizations have an unspoken (and unwritten) norm for avoiding open conflicts, instead resolving them behind closed doors.
- *Informal networks.* These are positive patterns of relationships between people that may be based on knowledge-sharing, trust, energy, or other characteristics. Savvy people—the

ones others seek out for their insight—are often called *hubs,* and these go-to people play critical roles in forming and maintaining informal networks. To envision one of your networks, consider the people you go to outside the normal hierarchy for career advice, political wisdom, or special expertise. Or the ones you share speculations with about "what is really going on here" when uncertainties prevail.

- *Communities.* These are more focused, cross-functional groups that share a common identity and practice. In some ways, a community is a more bounded network with a higher density of intergroup relationships, in addition to a common focus or reason for existence. One example might be a community focused on environmentally sustainable ways to do business. Another might be cigarette smokers who convene and interact daily in the designated outdoor smoking areas. A third might be minority groups who provide each other with informal support and mentorship.

- *Pride.* People feel proud when they use their skills to realize goals that are meaningful to them. The goals vary by individual. For example, a CEO may be proud of closing the latest acquisition deal, while a service representative may be equally proud of solving a loyal customer's complaint. Pride, and the anticipation of feeling pride, is a strong behavioral motivator. The pride is deepened when accomplishments are valued by people the worker respects outside the workplace, such as family members or mentors. Their approbation multiplies the motivational impact.

It can be an advantage that the informal elements are not written down and fixed. For example, it's easier to try new things when the rules are not rigidly codified. Networks and communities spring up faster when fueled by peer interactions within the informal organization than when ordered with an edict from the top. A sales rep who gets a spontaneous accolade from a customer feels far more pride—and more immediately—than any formal metric or monthly tracking system could inspire.

Sometimes we're asked if there is a difference between the informal organization and culture. It's a good question because the two have common elements and therefore can seem to be the same, but there is an important distinction. Our desk dictionary (*Merriam-Webster's Collegiate,* 10th edition) provides a good definition of culture as "the set of shared attitudes, values, goals and practices that characterizes (human behaviors in) a company or corporation." This definition, which we and many leaders would agree with, puts human behaviors at the center of culture, and human behaviors always involve both rational and emotional dimensions, as well as formal and informal components. Culture can also be more simply and colloquially described as "the way things are done around here."

The informal organization is better described by its mechanisms, most of which can be clearly identified and consciously influenced, and that link very closely with other cultural elements. Charlie Stewart's men, for example, had an informal mechanism for keeping him informed about fluid situations that enabled him to perform effectively when the time came. The mechanism no doubt developed over time as a result of the intense loyalty that Stewart and his men felt for each other.

It is difficult, if not impossible, to change a culture directly by trying to mandate a change in values like loyalty. It would not work, for example, to command Inskeep's men to be more loyal to each other. What does that mean? How does one go about doing that? However, had Inskeep been as sensitive as Stewart was in developing specific mechanisms that built emotional commitment among his men, they would have never let him down by not letting him know about the change in "salute plans."

Culture change can be effected, therefore, by adjusting the mechanisms of the informal organization in ways that tap into the underlying elements of human behaviors and result in the desired performance improvements. While programmatic change efforts driven through the formal organization can also change culture, they do so much more slowly and often with undesirable side effects from negative reactions and resistance to being programmed.

Unlike the formal, the informal construct is *not* strategic, analytical, logical, efficient, or enforceable. Nor is it manageable in the usual sense of that term. It is intuitive, personal, emotional, immediate—and it can be influenced. It is uniquely good for motivating people to go above and beyond their job duties, communicating information quickly and meaningfully, catalyzing collaboration, and accelerating behavior change. What exists outside the lines isn't as clearly defined as what exists within the lines.

THE ORGANIZATIONAL QUOTIENT

The Spanish bank Caja Navarra—known as CAN—has pioneered a new business model called "civic banking" that weds profit with social responsibility. The informal played an important role in enabling the company's CEO to transform what had been a typical, hierarchical Spanish community bank. For example, CAN hires people who do not have typical banking experience and places as much emphasis on their ability to work with customers as on their technical banking skills. The bank encourages employees to define their roles more broadly than as the collection of the tasks required in their formal positions. The focus on customers and civic service leads to the creation of informal networks both within the company and with people in the outside community. As a result, CAN has achieved real and positive social impact along with healthy profits.

Although Caja Navarra helped create its transformation through the informal organization, that does not mean that it abandoned its formal processes and practices. No bank could survive without them, after all.

In fact, the employees who are most effective in any organization invariably recognize the importance of both the formal and informal. People who take on a new position, in particular, find that the best way to succeed is to get smart quickly about how the informal side of an organization *actually* works rather than learning the formal processes governing how things are *supposed* to work. Some companies, like CAN and Google and Southwest Airlines, make this intuitive capability to sense the informal a criterion for new hires.

The characteristics of the formal and informal organizations can be compared to the differences between the traditional measure of intellectual ability, the intelligence quotient or IQ, and the emotional intelligence quotient or EQ. IQ purports to measure a person's rational skills and intellect through a battery of verbal and numerical performance tests. In school, students with high IQs tend to perform well and then attend prestigious institutions of higher learning, from which they move to careers requiring "book smarts." Most of the activities in the formal organization involve IQ skills: forming strategies, analyzing processes, designing structures, and creating integrated performance metrics.

However, it has long been argued that IQ does not measure all aspects of intelligence. In the past ten years in particular, the idea of emotional intelligence, or EQ, has gained currency in management thinking, largely thanks to the book of the same name by Daniel Goleman.[8] The origins of the concept, however, go back to Charles Darwin's work on the importance of emotional expression for survival. Darwin realized that empathy became an evolutionary advantage for primates because it greases the wheels of sociability. In the 1920s, Edward Thorndike, a professor at Columbia University, coined the phrase "social intelligence," which he described as the ability to understand and manage people.[9]

Goleman's book made such an impact, in the United States and around the world, that he expanded the concept to the workplace in his second book, *Working with Emotional Intelligence.* He writes, "The rules for work are changing. We're being judged by a new yardstick: not just by how smart we are, or by our training and expertise, but also by how well we handle ourselves and each other."[10]

IQ comes into play in the world of strategies, structures, and metrics. EQ is necessary to instill values, build relationships, and emotionally engage people with their work. A manager—indeed, any employee—can achieve extraordinary performance by knowing when to draw on IQ and when to employ EQ. Those who can do this have what we call a high "organizational quotient," or OQ. The ability to achieve this balance distinguishes the best managers from the formalists (who are highly reliant on IQ) and informalists or "relationship cultivators," who are much stronger in EQ.

KNOWING WHEN TO EMPHASIZE LOGIC OR MAGIC

The formal is best used for predictable and repeatable work that needs to be done efficiently and with little variance. The predictability and repeatability of the work warrants the effort to develop the infrastructure of the formal organization, which can be documented and constantly improved upon to improve efficiency and remove variation. Payroll distributions are a good example.

Conversely, the informal is best applied against unpredictable events. Issues that arise outside the scope of the formal organization are often surprises that need to be sensed and solved. Increasingly, people who need to do the solving need to be motivated outside the reward system, collaborate across organizational boundaries, and make decisions with little guidance from formal strategies. In many cases, activity in the informal organization starts to repeat itself, which is a signal for broader changes that need to be made to the formal organization.

Another distinction is that the formal organization is typically constrained by the doctrine of "best practice." A common desire across all organizations is the relentless pursuit of best practice as a means of improving performance in various functions, departments, and levels of management. The theory is simple: "If we can determine and apply proven best practices, we should be able to perform at the top level in our industry." However, great leaders are seldom satisfied with the formal spreading of best practices. And to go beyond best practice requires a level of insight, risk taking, and trial-and-error responsiveness that demands understanding and harnessing of the informal. This is often the magic that separates "best performance" from "best practice."

Characteristics of the Formal and the Informal

Formal	Informal
Efficient	Adaptive
Scalable	Local
Predictable	Innovative
Controlling	Motivating
Clear	Ambiguous
Disciplined	Spontaneous
Hierarchical	Collaborative
Rational	Emotional

2

When the Balance Shifts

L et's think about your customer, the do-it-yourselfer," Bernie
Marcus would tell his class of The Home Depot trainees, according to Chris Roush in his book, *Inside Home Depot*. Bernie goes on to
describe how the customer drives for several miles to reach the store
and has to park a long way from the entrance. He wanders the aisles
searching for a specific nut, but when he gets to where he's bought
the item before, he can't find what he wants. "You just screwed the
customer!" Bernie says.[1]

When Bernie Marcus and Arthur Blank founded The Home
Depot they fervently desired to serve their customers, not screw
them. And they believed the best way not to screw customers was
to not screw their employees—as the two believed they had been
screwed by their former bosses. Originally Bernie and Arthur had
been managers at Handy Dan's, one of the first do-it-yourself home
improvement chains in the United States.

Partly as a result of that experience, The Home Depot started
life as an enterprise decidedly tilted toward the human element.
"Bernie and I founded The Home Depot with a special vision,"
wrote Arthur Blank, "to create a company that would keep alive
the values that were important to us. Values like respect among all

people, excellent customer service, and giving back to our communities and society. And here is the key—a value only means something when you live it."

Bernie Marcus and Arthur Blank—Bernie, in particular—were masters at mobilizing the informal elements of the organization, although they did not necessarily describe their approach in those terms. At The Home Depot, employees were encouraged to work together, as well as build personal relationships and participate in social networks that were based on trust, respect, and common interests. Through rigorous training as well as the personal example of the founders, employees were urged to get to know each other personally, rather than as cogs in the system, and to learn about their customers as individuals, rather than as sales targets.

The culture drew on more than just a willingness to help out; it drew on an intimate understanding of the subtleties of home supply that enabled its people to empathize and form personal connections with their customers. So rigorous employee training dictated that everyone know the business inside and out. One former Home Depot executive whom we'll call Henry told us about his first three weeks on the job. He spent no time in the executive suite. Rather, he visited store after store, donning the famous orange apron in each one, working on the front line with everyone else.

Henry told us about his time at a store in California, where one day a supervisor asked him, "Henry, do you know how to operate a PB24?"

"Ah. No. I don't think so," Henry replied. "But I'm willing to learn."

"Good," said the supervisor. "Come with me."

Henry followed the supervisor into the kitchen department and stopped in the cleaning tools aisle. The supervisor removed a broom from the display and handed it to Henry.

"Push-Broom 24," the supervisor said with a smile. "See if you can make it work on this aisle." And so Henry, newly hired vice president, spent the next hour learning the features and benefits of the PB24. As a result of this experience, and the others he had in Home Depot stores, Henry gained a great deal of knowledge about the nitty-gritty of being a frontline employee for the company.

Employees took such pride in their orange aprons and their expert knowledge that The Home Depot "way" became widely known, with mordant humor, as Agent Orange. Employees did not think of their jobs as work, they thought of them as a calling. One employee we interviewed in a Home Depot in Atlanta said, in effect, "Don't tell my husband, but I would really rather come in here to work on the weekend than face the drudgery at home— it's much more enjoyable. I love the work, the people, and the customers!"

This is not to say that The Home Depot did not have its formal processes and procedures. In fact, Arthur Blank was a dyed-in-the-wool formalist. Trained as an accountant, he was known for his devotion to charts and spreadsheets and his ability to discuss the intricacies of pricing and overhead in great detail. In his training sessions with employees, he reveled in such questions as, "Would it be more valuable for a Home Depot lumber department to hire one person who had six years of experience as a carpenter at $10 an hour or to hire two people for $5 an hour who had once framed a house?" Answer: It all depends on what the store, and, more important, on what its customers need. In other words, the formal aspects of the company were in service of the informal ones.

Thanks to the great service and committed employees—as well as huge selection, low pricing, and convenient locations—Bernie and Arthur's venture skyrocketed into the most successful retail building materials chain in history.

MAKE WAY FOR MR. NARDELLI

For many years, The Home Depot grew and prospered, driven by its informal organization—values, people, attitudes, habits, behaviors, stories.

But as the company grew, it became more complex and diverse. More structure, process, and program consistency was needed to balance the rather loose processes of Agent Orange. Bernie Marcus retired from active participation in the company and Arthur Blank took the reins. One might have expected that Blank would have led a shift to the formal and that The Home Depot's growth would continue. Instead, the company's profit margin and market share began to slide. What had looked like an unstoppable rise of the greatest retailer in America suddenly appeared stalled.

Not surprisingly, The Home Depot's board grew increasingly concerned about the company's future. They concluded that they needed a clearer strategy along with more disciplined management, and, above all, a new CEO. They recruited Robert Nardelli, a former president and senior executive at General Electric. To most informed observers, Nardelli was the best possible choice. GE executives are known for their strategic rigor, organizational clarity, and analytic discipline. Just what The Home Depot needed.

True to form, Nardelli immediately pursued ways to cut costs and improve efficiency. For example, inventory is a major issue at a huge retailer like The Home Depot. Since Nardelli came from a manufacturing business that had also depended on smart management of inventory, he focused early attention on disciplined inventory processes. But he had been dealing with business customers who placed large orders on regular schedules and whose needs were relatively predictable. They were, in short, quite rational.

Retail customers, however, are far less predictable and much more emotionally driven. As Marcus taught in his story about the missing nut, customers hate stockouts. The consequences of too many failures to supply what customers demand can be catastrophic. Increasingly, they had other suppliers to choose from—if The Home Depot didn't have what they needed, Lowe's, Costco, or even the corner hardware store might.

One of the great strengths of The Home Depot's founders had been their intuitive feel for supply and demand variables. Years in the business made them extremely good at determining how much inventory would be needed in different categories of goods at different times of the year, and they would order accordingly.

Our executive friend Henry provided an example of the vagaries of the home building supply business and their effect on inventory. Now and again, Henry told us, an electrician would come in to his local Home Depot to buy forty units of fluorescent lighting. He would never call ahead to see if the units were in stock. He would never place an order. He would just show up intending to buy whatever number of lighting fixtures he needed for the job he was working on at the time. The store employees knew the electrician and his habits so they were almost always able to fulfill his needs.

It's very difficult to fit this kind of intermittent purchase into the kind of formal inventory tracking system that Nardelli and his efficiency experts were installing throughout The Home Depot empire. The managers still knew that the electrician would show up with his big order, but they were now handcuffed by an inventory system that dictated how many units they could stock, based on the average flow of sales over time.

Inevitably, the day came when the electrician walked in, strode to the aisle he had visited dozens of times before, and found only ten units available. The first time it happened, he mentioned it to the manager. The second time, he drove down the street to another home supply store. There was no third time.

The inventory controls made economic sense—they were per-fectly logical—but they did not account for the sense of pride that store personnel took in serving their local customers and commu-nities. Nor could the system track the lost sales or the number of customers who walked out disappointed.

Nardelli no doubt believed that his cost-cutting and efficiency-improvement measures would put some formal backbone into what was an overly informal organization. However, rather than creating balance, his shifts disturbed it. As Henry acknowledges, there was a trade-off—efficiency took precedence over effectiveness. "When the E's flipped," Henry says, "the wheels came off pretty fast." Despite a boom in the housing and home improvement markets, the compa-ny's stock price remained relatively sluggish during Nardelli's tenure, while the stock of competitor Lowe's soared.

Nardelli was not wrong to cut costs and find ways to improve efficiency. Nor was he wrong to assume that the inefficiencies in the system had come about largely because of the informal ways of Agent Orange. However, the problem was that Nardelli did little to mobilize the informal organization in support of what he was try-ing to do. No doubt employees knew very well that their company needed better systems and more rigor. They might very well have supported Nardelli's initiatives if he had sought to enlist the infor-mal in the cause.

The Formal and Informal Are Intertwined

Earlier we described the polarized view that many management the-orists take toward the formal and informal organizations, but not all of them have been so aligned with one side or the other.

One person, Chester Barnard, stood out from the crowd in understanding how the rational and emotional interact in the workplace, and his work and wisdom now seem to have been well ahead of their time. A decade before "the happiness boys" hit MIT, Barnard not only explained that organizations were both rational and emotional, he also defined the terms *informal* and *formal organization*— one of the first business thinkers to do so. Unlike many of the theorists we cited earlier, Barnard spent most of his career as an executive: he worked for nearly forty years at the American Telephone and Telegraph Company, completing his career as president of the New Jersey Bell Telephone Company. He was also unusually active in public service as president of the Rockefeller Foundation, chairman of the National Science Foundation, and an assistant to the Secretary of the Treasury.

In 1938, Barnard published *The Functions of the Executive,* in which he defined the concept of the formal and informal organization and the relationship between the two. He wrote, "When we undertake to persuade others to do what we wish, we assume that they are able to decide whether they will or not. . . . When we make rules, regulations, laws—which we deliberately do in great quantities—we assume generally that as respects their subject matter those affected by them are governed by forces outside themselves."[2]

Barnard's theory is that formal mechanisms (rules) rob us of choice, while the informal mechanisms (persuasion) necessitate choice. For example, a rule of submitting receipts for over $25 removes the choice not to. A value of "spend money wisely" necessitates a choice around what spending limit is considered wise. In short, he recognized that the informal forces that necessitate choice and the formal rules that restrict it are related. In this book, we use the term *balance* to get at this relationship. But by this we do not mean that the informal and formal are present in equal measure. Rather, we mean that their relative influence on people's choices and behaviors in an organization is appropriate for the performance outcomes that are expected from them.

The Home Depot story, for example, shows how the formal and informal need to be balanced in a very particular way that enables a company to draw on the best of both—although not necessarily in equal measure—to achieve superior performance.

In general, the formal organization is best at handling clear-cut situations, known tasks, well-defined relationships, and standardized transactions. Many of these formal processes and tasks can be automated and have been over the years. Emotions, personal relationships, and individual abilities do not play a large role. Because of this, the formal organization can be fine-tuned to operate with great efficiency and consistency.

The strengths of the informal organization do not really show in the established routine of everyday company business. Rather, they show their value when unexpected or new situations arise, when work needs to be done across boundaries, when specifications are unclear, or when changes must be made. Almost every organization must deal with both predictable and unpredictable work. This is one of the reasons it is necessary to learn how and when to call on the logic of the formal and balance it with the magic of the informal.

In its early years, Starbucks achieved this balance well. Howard Shultz, the company's former CEO and current chairman, did an excellent job of building and fostering the informal organization, but he also recognized that the formal element must play a key role. In a *Fast Company* article, he is quoted as saying, "You can't grow if you're driven only by process, or only by the creative spirit. You've got to achieve a fragile balance between the two sides of the corporate brain."[3]

The Starbucks commitment to balancing the formal and informal is demonstrated in its approach to training its frontline workforce—the "baristas" or "partners" (the Starbucks term for employees). There are guiding principles that help Starbucks partners make the right decisions, but there are no scripts or ironclad rules that govern their behavior. Starbucks focuses on building partners' confidence so that the majority of decisions can be made at or near the front line and in real time, without constantly sending decisions upward.

This early balance between formal and informal helped Starbucks accomplish the performance objective of ensuring sufficient consistency. For example, a customer's favorite half-caf vanilla grande latte will taste the same in Concord as in Charleston as in New York. This balance also ensures that employees don't become automatons.

And when we say the balance matters in every organization, we do not mean just business enterprises. To make the point, here is a story set as far from the world of business as anything we can imagine. Nonetheless, it illustrates both the diversity and timelessness of this relationship.

Balance Matters Even in the African Bush

The !Kung bushmen of southern Africa have developed an intriguing balance between the formal and informal organizations. (The !Kung speak a language that uses a click sound before some consonants, and the click is often denoted with a ! in text. We should also say that we have not worked directly with the !Kung people, so our understanding of them is based on secondary sources.)

The !Kung is a hunter-gatherer society in Namibia and Botswana. The group makes no permanent settlements. Its people constantly travel across the plains and camp wherever their search for food takes them. Not surprisingly, they have few material possessions.

The !Kung do, however, have the equivalent of a formal organization. The most stable social unit is the immediate family, consisting of a husband, wife (or wives), and children. Bands consisting of an extended family of about twenty people stay together and perform certain defined and repeated functions, including building temporary shelters, cooking meals, making clothing and tools, maintaining spears and replenishing supplies of poison-tipped arrows, keeping a fire constantly burning, and tending the children. These bands are less rigid, often breaking up and recombining as the structure of single families change, but a new band will generally attend to the same tasks as the old.

Although the !Kung's formal organization structure handles these regular responsibilities with consistency and efficiency, the group lives in a highly unstable environment. People do not know exactly where they will find game or vegetation. The weather is unpredictable and often extreme. The group is subject to accidents and disease. Water supplies are uncertain.

To handle these situations, the !Kung rely on their informal organization. For the unpredictable jobs of hunting game and gathering food, they form smaller groups of six to ten people who develop skill sets suited to the particular kind of game they're stalking or the characteristics of the landscape they're in. Some are expert in the medicinal or toxic properties of various plants. Others have particular skills at killing birds, others at capturing giraffes. Women tend to track small mammals. Men go after the wildebeest.

In even more dire circumstances, the !Kung will also go outside the boundaries of their formal structure, tapping into larger networks of other bands and groups when resources are very scarce or they lose members to disease or death. They quickly create informal networks to pool and distribute resources. The more unusual the circumstances, the more broadly the !Kung will tap into diverse networks to form new groupings.

Maintaining this balance is everyone's job. However, the job is always changing. Managing the range of jobs, from predictable to unpredictable, is a lot easier when you can access both formal and informal mechanisms to fit the situation.

An Ever-Changing Balance Point

The balance of the formal and informal changes over the course of a company's life cycle and imbalances tend to appear during periods of significant growth—or significant declines in growth.

Young companies, those with between ten and fifty people, are informal by nature for four very good reasons. First, their worlds are largely unpredictable and unstable. Second, the participants know each other personally. Third, they are constantly forming and reforming in different ways to address sudden unexpected challenges. Finally, the personal values of the company are usually strongly shared—even if unstated—because of the hands-on involvement of leaders and the visible, interactive way they make decisions and solve problems on the run.

In these companies, productive relationships develop organically through long hours, shared space, and collective frustrations. Such relationships usually reflect mutual respect, common interests, a strong sense of purpose, and feelings of pride in working together to accomplish that purpose; these are natural motivators for the emerging enterprise. Who needs the cumbersome formal stuff?

As the organization grows, however, it increasingly needs to create distinct work groups, clear structures, and repeatable workflow processes. For example, in technology start-ups, the introduction of a sales function is often the first shock to the homogeneity of the engineering culture. The sales function may be less invested in the cool technology and more focused on how to meet customers' needs. Given that sales skills are more fungible than technical skills in an organization of modest size, competitive compensation becomes more important to attract, motivate, and retain the sales force. Similarly, as operations scale up to handle mass manufacturing rather than small-batch prototypes, the management of quality control metrics becomes more important. As the organization grows,

so does the need for clarity around who is responsible and accountable for execution, who has decision-making authority, and who
controls resources. The growing complexity of work flows amplifies
the need for lucid processes that add direction and efficiency for
work that is repeated often. As complexity increases, tough leaders
demand more clarity about who deserves credit or blame.

The increases in need for formal elements (compensation plans,
operational controls, clarity of accountability and responsibility, and
efficient work flows), can happen gradually or in waves. Generally,
by the time a company organization has surpassed a thousand people, it needs a robust and coordinated formal organization. At that
point, without reasonable clarity of structure and rules, behavioral
alignment is difficult to sustain in the large groups required, and the
lack of formal organization can lead to confusion, frustration, and a
sense of futility.

As the organization continues to grow, new waves of professional managers derive increasing performance benefits from the
formal system. More robust strategic planning, enterprise-wide processes, and consistently cascading scorecards for measuring performance help the organization obtain scale advantages from its size.
Efficiency programs are a hallmark of this stage.

The informal organization still plays a critical role throughout, though not always a positive one. In fact, the informal is what
largely determines the acceptance or rejection of new formal initiatives, as in The Home Depot story. It can slow things down or speed
things up. However, as it garners less and less leadership attention,
the informal fades into the background. This can be the most difficult time to maintain the benefits of an effective informal organization. Unless leaders choose their formal actions carefully, they can
inadvertently alienate powerful informal elements.

The evaporation of attention to the informal is often manifest
in various, and worrisome, performance problems. Many leaders are

unable to pinpoint the informal root of the problem (such as loss of trust). This problem can be triggered by fear that the organization is losing touch with customers, facing a radically different and antagonistic marketplace, or is operationally unsustainable.

Often the formal changes needed for business development are actually strangling the informal, which slowly weakens as the company grows. In *What Got You Here Won't Get You There,* executive coach Marshall Goldsmith writes that the balance between the informal and formal characteristics that help a leader achieve success in one stage of growth is not necessarily the right balance for the next stage.[4] Just as organizations that have grown organically and informally will need to add more formal processes, leaders also need to become increasingly conscious of the changing role of the informal organization, giving it the attention and resources it needs to stay healthy and supportive.

Like any fast-growing, successful enterprise, eBay had to constantly monitor and manage the balance. Its business was originally built on its enormous community of millions of buyers and sellers who exchange goods and money. eBay maintained a light touch in monitoring and enforcing ethical behavior by its customers—the entire enterprise relied on transparency and collective trust in good intentions. In the early days, there was almost no retribution for breaking that trust, other than bad seller ratings, which warned fellow eBay-ers away from doing business with those who broke the rules. For both the founders and the early eBay community, this openness and free market philosophy were the foundation of what made eBay so popular. The company culture was modeled on this sense of trust among the rapidly expanding community of users—it was often described as a nonhierarchical, democratic organization.

But as the company got bigger, the exponential growth of its user base led to more and more cases where the rules were egregiously broken. At a certain point, eBay's CEO Meg Whitman recognized that formal mechanisms were needed to protect the vast majority of eBay-ers who were good-willed and to safeguard the health of the company.

So, in 1999, Rob Chesnut, a former federal prosecutor, was hired to run a newly formed department called Rules, Trust, and Safety. Chesnut established a number of new policies to help protect against fraud and also to formally address behaviors that were out of step with the eBay community's values but that had proved to be very difficult to self-police. That same year, the company decided to ban selling of firearms on its site. "Having them up there just wasn't appropriate," Whitman said in a November 2001 *Fast Company* article. "It didn't fit with the kind of company we wanted to be."[5]

While the existence of an ever-changing balance point between formal and informal seems obvious to us now, it took a while for us to see it.

If You Can Make It Here: How Katz Learned About Balance

Katz learned directly from his stint in the Navy how important and powerful the informal organization can be, but did not yet understand the importance of balancing both the formal and informal. He became convinced that the informal was the best way to ensure cross-organization collaboration, emotional commitment and motivation, real team performance, flexibility, and responsiveness. That was such a valuable lesson that he came to assume that the informal was much more important than the formal in *every* organization and changed his style to take full advantage of it.

A few years after Katz got out of the Navy, he was the managing director of the San Francisco office of McKinsey & Company. In that role, he left the formal organization almost entirely to others and focused his attention on the informal elements of teaming, emotional commitment, and informal networking that he had mastered on the USS *Nicholas*.

Because it was a relatively small office (about thirty-five consultants plus an equal number of support staff) the approach worked pretty well. The other partners often functioned as a real team, the informal networks usually produced responsive collaboration and strong emotional commitment. Most important, the staff was highly motivated by pride in what they did, how they did it, and why.

The San Francisco office performed well enough that Katz was promoted (or so they called it) to run McKinsey's office in New York City. By that time, he considered himself a "master of the informal," and, since he had been so successful in San Francisco, he set out to apply his knowledge of the informal to the new assignment. But Katz was managing four times the number of people in New York as he had been in San Francisco and, instead of the collaboration and commitment that had developed there, his methods produced frustration and unrest among the partners, an erosion of the discipline required for real teamwork, and a drop in performance.

It took two years for it to become obvious that the informal-formal balance that had worked so well in San Francisco was not right for New York and could not create, much less sustain, higher levels of performance. Katz was replaced as manager of the office and moved along to a new assignment at McKinsey. It was a painful experience for Katz, but an invaluable one, since he says he usually learns more from failures than from successes.

• • • • • • • • •

So the discovery of the informal needs to be balanced with the recognition that appropriate elements of the formal are equally important, particularly as size and complexity increases. An obvious point? Maybe, but many leaders and their companies still don't seem to get the balance right.

3

Jumping Together

E. O. Wilson, the great American naturalist, has a lot to say about the importance of bringing together the formal and the informal, even if he doesn't quite describe it that way. In *Consilience: The Unity of Knowledge,* he writes about how we can integrate the different sciences and might, eventually, even be able to integrate the sciences with the humanities.[1]

That's an admirable aspiration and one well worth pursuing! But what exactly does that word *consilience* mean? According to the *Oxford English Dictionary*, its definitions include "agreeing," "concurrence," and, our personal favorite, "jumping together." This is not quite as easy as it might sound.

In fact, the difficulty of getting the formal and informal organizations jumping together has been the subject of management theorists' work for at least a century. Mary Parker Follett, a pioneer in the study of organizations and a key figure in the human relations movement, defined the notion of integration as early as the 1920s, by saying, "When two [conflicting] desires are integrated, that means that a solution has been found in which both desires have found a place, that neither side has had to sacrifice anything."[2]

Thus leading outside the lines need not diminish the impact of leading inside the lines. Indeed, when the actions are integrated, the lines largely vanish and "leading" becomes a holistic style that moves organizations to places they couldn't otherwise go.

The Informal Is the Underdog

Most managers would love to get the formal and informal aspects of their companies jumping together, so why is it so hard to do?

One reason is that the informal is so much harder to recognize, control, and quantify than the formal. Another is that the predominant management mindset encourages people to emphasize formal control and pursue rational paths based upon logical (typically analytical) reasoning. And a third reason—perhaps the most insidious—is that leadership development programs tend to reward and advance those who excel at rigor, process efficiency, and hierarchical control.

Invisibility of the Informal

Executives tend to favor the formal organization because it can be easily understood and explicitly described. It's relatively easy to specify who reports to whom and where decisions are officially made.

Many executives think of the informal organization as the opposite of the formal, a mysterious connection of underground interactions, many of which are distracting (at the very least) and probably downright counterproductive—little more than a rumor mill that operates beneath the radar. Their hope is that the informal, if left alone, will follow the lead of the formal. Or if not, the formal will somehow drag the informal along.

The differences in visibility between the formal and informal come into play most obviously when a new person joins the organization. It is a relatively straightforward matter to get the incoming employee up to speed on the formal organization, but the informal has to be experienced to be understood. Reading the official values statement does not enable one to understand how shared values really play out in an organization. The org chart does not include all the players who need to be part of the decision-making process, nor does it show the back channels of advice giving and trust seeking (or undermining) that influence decisions. New people often struggle with this invisibility, and those with a low organizational quotient find themselves frustrated and struggling long after colleagues with higher OQ have learned the ropes.

Intractability of Prevalent Mindsets

The informal organization is difficult for many leaders to comprehend, largely because the prevalent management mindsets are based on very different and more powerful images, particularly *business-as-war* and *business-as-science*.

The warrior-manager views organizational groups as akin to military combat units. Competitors are the enemies and the name of the game is to conquer them. To do so requires discipline and control mechanisms not unlike those used by the armed services.

As Karl Weick, the organizational theorist, pointed out, military terms are widely used in the language of business.[3] Headquarters, chief officer, staff, front line, divisions, strategy, tactics, recruiting, competitive intelligence, discipline, codes of conduct, and rules of engagement are all common terms in corporate vocabularies. The business-as-war mindset implies a natural hierarchy, where strategic choices are made at the top, tactical actions are executed from the middle, and heroic and unquestioning individual performance is expected at the front line. This mindset reveres controlled and efficient execution. Many managers, like many military officers, do not like unpredictability in their fields of operations. Surprises are almost always viewed as a bad thing because they disrupt the controls that are meant to establish and maintain order. Eliminating variances, getting back to plan, and delivering predicted results are highly valued outcomes of a well-designed formal organization. We have all seen exciting new opportunities get under-resourced because there were no funds from the annual budget to support them—even if that budget was developed a year ago under very different conditions.

This mindset is so deeply ingrained in the business world that managers rarely notice it. We worked with one company in the telecommunications industry to help its thirty top executives diagnose their culture. As Zia opened the session he made a comment about the business-as-war mindset and how this particular company had a command-and-control approach that was reflected in the military expressions that were broadly used throughout the organization. Everyone thought that was a valuable insight. Lots of head nodding and affirmative murmurs.

When our work was complete, we wrote a report that included the same insight. The president of the company was not amused. "The use of military terms reflects the behavior of only a small minority in this company," she told us. "And that behavior does *not* fit our culture."

After some further discussion about how inappropriate the military behavior was to the values of the company, the president became quite agitated. "In fact," she said, "I think the only solution is to bomb that minority right out of here." We did not detect any irony in her tone of voice.

Warrior-managers tend to focus very sharply on the formal organization, in three important ways.

First, they overemphasize the importance of marching in step to execute a plan instead of improvising in the moment as things develop. (They persist in this even though the most successful generals argue that it is impossible and even unwise to follow a battle plan once the action starts. Marines, for example, are urged to "always follow the intent" of the leader two levels up whenever a battle situation is inconsistent with the orders from the immediate next in command.)

Second, their emphasis on defined hierarchy and structure results in sharply defined boundaries between "us" and "them"—whether the "them" belong to internal groups or are outside the organization. This attachment to the idea of formal boundaries often gets in the way of informal relationships, collaborations, and networks, which are highly fluid in nature.

Third, warrior-managers tend to overemphasize the importance of formal position, and assume that people will shoulder work and take on responsibility based solely on their rank and authority. In doing so, they overlook the most important motivator of discretionary efforts to achieve performance: feeling good about the day-to-day work itself.

While the business-as-war concept concentrates on how power flows through structures and processes, the business-as-science mindset concentrates on how problems are solved. Many conference rooms, project charters, and program descriptions are dominated by the logical language of models, proofs, hypotheses, and data analysis. This reflects a belief in the ultimate power of rational analysis to solve problems and develop solutions.

This mindset appeals to scientist-managers because it implies an objectively right answer to any question, as long as rigorous analytic and scientific methods are employed. This mindset further implies that only a select few minds and experienced leaders can be trusted to determine these rational truths: those who have the appropriate levels of intellect, experience, and training, and who occupy the appropriate formal roles. Like priests in ancient temples, strategic planning groups, MBA-adorned executives, and specialist consultants hold considerable sway in determining objective truth for the broader organization.

The Enron debacle provides a classic illustration of how a business-as-science mindset can inhibit the positive influence of the informal organization. When this happens to the degree it did at Enron, it can foster the kind of self-serving elitism that subverts, subordinates, and ignores warning signals and wisdom from truly insightful people down the line.

Not long before the Enron story broke in October of 2001, we did an analysis of the company's latest employee survey. It showed that employees felt there was a big gap between the company's financial performance and its vision, values, and employee commitment. The formal structure (and the so-called superior logic of the strategy) dominated the informal organization so completely that lapses in ethics and behaviors that were inconsistent with the values went unchecked.

The business-as-science mindset influences leaders in two important ways. First, it overemphasizes the rational compared to the emotional and de-emphasizes the value of intuition and wisdom. Not only can this lead to incomplete or suboptimal solutions, it can also virtually ensure that those solutions will not be fully committed to and executed with energy over time.

Second, it focuses the problem-solving responsibility on too few people because of their formal status, perceived insight, and rational judgment. Important problems are solved every day by people throughout the organization, and the role of leaders increasingly needs to be about enabling and incorporating that broad-based problem solving into the leadership system, rather than paying serious attention only to the problem solving of a few smart senior people.

Leadership Programs Favor the Formal

The systems that companies use to attract, select, develop, and promote leaders are formal processes. They focus on templates and skills necessary to managing the formal organization—and thus create a self-reinforcing system that rewards formalists.

The informal organization has its own way of attracting, selecting, developing, and rewarding people—but it rarely has the power to affect promotion or compensation. Therefore, those who rise to influential positions in the hierarchy are more likely to be more comfortable with and skilled at using the formal organization than the informal. And they are the ones most likely to shape the leadership development process.

The selection of leaders is often based on qualifications that can be demonstrated on a résumé. These are sometimes skill-based (for example, certifications and academic degrees), or based on some quantifiable accomplishment (increased sales by 20 percent), or experience-based (succeeded in a diversity of formal roles).

Informal leaders rarely have the kind of explicit qualifications that can be easily documented or communicated, much less evaluated. In fact, we find that the masters of the informal organization are close to the front line, and (somewhat surprisingly) seldom seen as high-potential fast-tracking candidates for top leadership roles.

Sometimes referred to as the B players, they are not typically in hot pursuit of rapid promotions and have only limited influence over the compensation and advancement of their people.[4] Nonetheless, they play a critical if unrecognized role in the organization's performance. But their primary source of motivation has to come from informal sources. Not surprisingly, the further up the organizational ladder one climbs, the more one relies on the formal elements, and the more one lets the informal elements fade into the background.

The training of leaders is more centered on the formal skills and experiences required to manage the formal organization, such as constructing a solid business case, communicating logically, evaluating measurable performance, working in formal roles, and managing project time lines.

To be fair, many human resource people recognize the importance of training leaders in the ways of the informal organization. But all too often this training is disconnected from business performance, so that the link between the soft skills and financial performance is obscured. For example, training in team leadership seldom highlights the fact that the primary (perhaps the only) motivator of team performance is the pride team members share in their team's composition, its working approach, and their common commitment to performance and results. Instead, would-be team leaders are encouraged to seek bonding, togetherness, and personal chemistry fits—measuring success by how well the group enjoys team-building offsites in the woods, rather than how often it exceeds its performance expectations.

• • • • • • • • •

So jumping together is a lot harder than it might sound. Yet the more admirable leaders and organizations do find ways to do it, much to their performance and competitive advantage. Not surprisingly, however, they often have to find their own path to get there.

ORPHEUS: A UNIQUE PATH TO INTEGRATION

The Orpheus Chamber Orchestra is one of the most startling examples of how an organization must find its own best way to get the formal and informal jumping together.

Orpheus is one of the leading classical orchestras in the world. Its recordings win Grammy awards and it holds frequent concerts at Carnegie Hall and other prestigious performance venues around the world. To listen to a recording of the orchestra, one might think it was just another group of world-class musicians. Without actually seeing a performance, the only difference one might notice between Orpheus and another orchestra is an extra quality of enthusiasm in the musicians' performance, as though they were all playing their favorite piece.

Only when observing the musicians live does the primary difference become clear. Orpheus is missing a central feature of virtually all other orchestras: a conductor. In other words, Orpheus succeeds without the most central element of the formal organization: the CEO.

An Early Emphasis on the Informal

Orpheus was founded by a group of musicians in 1972 and, from its beginning, the idea was that there would be no conductor. This unusual configuration for an orchestra of this size came about not as a reaction against the authority of the conductor, but as a statement of faith in the talent and commitment of its musicians.[5]

In a traditional orchestra, the conductor acts as a formal leader, the one who not only keeps individuals in time during a performance but also makes key decisions as the interpreter of the composer's vision, determining which moments in a piece need to be highlighted and which need a subtler touch. Musicians themselves, however, can often feel relegated to the role of cogs in a machine—expected to follow orders without the responsibility of determining how the music should be interpreted.

In Orpheus, every musician feels accountable for the decisions of the entire orchestra. The musicians rely on personal intuition, networks, individual commitment, and energy to stay together and listen for, or feel, group choices in musical interpretation. Ronnie Bauch, who was a violinist with Orpheus for many years, told us, "In traditional orchestras, there's a tentative quality. Performers kind of wait for their cues and directions from the conductor. In Orpheus, without a conductor, the musicians have to listen very intensely to one another. That means a much more active, far less passive, performance technique that creates a different, richer sound. The audience can really hear it."

Listening to Ronnie describe the early days at Orpheus, you can hear the nostalgia in his voice and see a knowing look in his eyes. At the outset, they were "experimenting with music," rehearsing for up to hundreds of hours for each concert, with much of this time spent debating what pieces should be performed and how they should be played. It was a kind of musical Petri dish, in which all the musicians were thrown together, trying to figure out how to grow a colony—where it was all for one and one for all. The sole formal element of the original Orpheus was a concertmaster, who acted as a temporary artistic director at each performance and who would mediate if there were disputes about interpretation or repertoire.

Although this overwhelmingly informal atmosphere produced great music, the musicians found that it was emotionally and physically draining, as well as very time-consuming for everyone involved. Orpheus placed great demands on its members, most of whom also had commitments to other orchestras and had their own recording and teaching schedules. Orpheus required a greater number of rehearsals than a traditional orchestra—and they were longer rehearsals. It took more time to determine the repertoire. And the discussions, which often escalated into arguments about interpretation, took a toll.

Burned out and frustrated, some of the best members of the orchestra began to leave.

Integrating a Formal Element into the Music

As Orpheus began to achieve more and more critical success and gain international attention, it became clear that the orchestra's often haphazard informal organization could no longer support the growing demand for its music and that it would face further attrition. It would have to find a more efficient system, one that would maintain the integrity of the music and the process without overburdening the players.

"It was like any business that moves out of its start-up phase," Ronnie says. "We realized we needed to institute a formal set of systems to meet our growing audience demand more consistently as a successful, stable organization."

Orpheus realized that the formal and informal were out of balance and that, without a stronger formal organization, the informal would begin to suffer. The musicians did not, however, wish to bring in a conductor. So to maintain a sense of shared leadership while increasing efficiency and improving decision making, they created a new process they called the "core system." A small group of elected leaders (the core) would be chosen when they began rehearsals for a new piece. It would include the concert master, the concert master's second, and a leader from each section of the orchestra.

Initially, the core would work through the piece—without the rest of the orchestra—to make decisions about how the piece should be played and to minimize the time required for full orchestra rehearsals. When the entire orchestra did meet, the core would lead the piece, although every musician was still able and expected to comment and ask questions. Since the core would change for each piece of music, and in each concert leadership responsibilities would rotate among numerous members of the orchestra, a spider web of informal networks between performers was created. For example, during a concert a violinist must listen for and connect with the concert master, the immediate section leader, the leaders of other sections, and the other members of the violin section.

The core system worked. It allowed Orpheus to retain shared leadership and still institute a formal structure to improve productivity and efficiency. Maintaining critical elements of the informal organization enables its people to do what seems highly counterintuitive, if not impossible—play beautiful music without a conductor. They have been able to sustain their unique approach while preserving their informal roots.

Building a Business Structure

As Orpheus gained critical acclaim (the orchestra won a Grammy in 1999), other organizational problems began to emerge. It went on longer international tours and expanded into new activities such as educational demonstrations that put new pressures on the members and the orchestra's resources. In an attempt to put in more professional management, an executive director was hired. The board, dissatisfied with his leadership, eventually stepped in and took control.

In December 2002, the board hired Graham Parker as general director—a new position whose responsibilities included marketing, operations, and tour management. Graham reported to Ronnie Bauch, who at the time was managing director. In 2008, as the orchestra began to face new and more complex financial challenges, Graham was promoted to executive director to clarify the leadership structure.

While administering an orchestra requires formal accountability and defined roles, all the business leaders at Orpheus are inspired by—and seek to follow the example of—the Orpheus philosophy. Just as the musicians share the tasks of leadership and commit themselves to the good of the whole organization, the administration thrives on its own informal organization. While there are formal elements of title and role, the administrators find that—when they are performing administrative functions at their peak level—everyone in the office operates with a kind of fluidity that is more characteristic of the informal.

In late 2007, Zia and Alex Goldsmith, one of our colleagues at Katzenbach Partners, began to work with Orpheus on a strategic planning effort. This came about because the orchestra had made plans to embark on a major capital campaign to build an endowment. Its administrators found that they did not have a sufficiently clear and compelling story about the orchestra's vision, mission, and long-range strategy to tell their potential donors. They made the assumption, however, that a traditional strategic planning process would not create a story that reflected their unique and highly informal culture.

So they conducted their planning sessions much like the musicians led their rehearsals. They created a facilitator group that functioned in a manner similar to that of the artistic director. It led the meetings and held ultimate decision-making rights. Then a core was chosen, whose members represented, in equal proportion, the musicians, staff members, and board members.

The collaborative aspects of the planning surfaced ideas and emotional commitment that top-down attempts at strategy could not. The formal structure—the core, facilitator group, and clear decision-making responsibility—ensured that the informality of the discussions did not slow things down or get in the way of taking action.

During the process, it became clear that the organization still had leadership challenges that needed to be solved. So the executive team took a little time out from the process, stepped back, and addressed the question of how the orchestra could maintain artistic creativity *and* run its operations more efficiently. Working with Richard Hackman, an Orpheus trustee and Harvard psychology professor, Orpheus introduced a senior leadership team, a unique leadership system that integrated their informal passion with formal clarity about accountabilities. In addition to the senior leadership team, artistic issues are largely dealt with in the artistic planning group, which consists of the artistic directors, the executive director, and general manager. Operational issues are dealt with in weekly staff meetings that Graham holds with the administrative staff.

The deliberate integration happens within the senior leadership team, which consists of Graham, the four administrative directors, and the lead artistic director. As Graham says, "We have a member of the orchestra at the table all the time, which produces positive tension. At a normal orchestra, you wouldn't have musicians sitting at the table with management. They would talk among themselves, then go speak to management. We have to talk about the issues right in front of each other."

The senior leadership team is very disciplined about constructing its meeting agendas to ensure that operational issues do not creep into the discussion and that there is enough time to explore broader topics. "It's a place where five of us can come together for two hours once a week and think, dream, and figure out how we move from here to there," Graham says. By deliberately mixing the two communities—managerial and artistic—within a formal structure, a tremendous amount of creativity is unleashed.

To bring this kind of structure to life, Graham realized that they would have to pay as much attention to *how* they worked together as they did to *what* they worked on. Their first all-day retreat was spent discussing, debating, and agreeing to behavioral norms. As Orpheus continues to face the challenges of growth and increasing renown, it will need to continue to depend on the kind of integrated formal and informal solutions that it has become very adept at finding.

THE ELEMENTS OF INTEGRATION

We generally use the word *balance* when we mean that the influences of the formal and informal mechanisms remain distinct but work together. We use the word *integrate* when we mean that the formal and informal mechanisms have somehow combined to achieve an overall influence where the distinct contributions of formal and informal are hard to separate. Don't worry too much about this distinction—it's a subtlety, but we want to be explicit for those who puzzle over these kinds of things.

Getting informal and formal mechanisms to integrate is tricky, and the shifting balance point between the informal and formal organization is but one part of this challenge. The inherent leadership bias to overrely on the formal, plus the inherent limitations of the informal, make for a very dynamic situation. However, when all parties keep an eye on the balance, as well as on jumping together, needs become clear and practical solutions present themselves. Of course there is a trial-and-error element to finding the right balance, but with experience the errors become less troublesome. Wise leaders learn how to monitor the line between the formal and informal organizations.

Whereas a process makes a certain set of work tasks efficient, underlying networks can help people quickly team up to solve issues that arise unexpectedly and therefore cannot be solved easily by a predetermined process. Integration is critical because, if there is one constant that high-performing organizations have to deal with, it is balance-disrupting change. So it is very important that leaders learn to spot important signposts that indicate integration is actually happening between formal and informal mechanisms. For example:

Emotionally motivated decisions and actions that align with strategic intent. People at all levels understand how company aspirations translate into their daily work. They are emotionally committed to, as well as rationally clear about, the critical aspects of their jobs, and act accordingly. Consider Southwest Airlines and how its employees—from pilots to baggage handlers—all pitch in to make sure planes take off on time. This is an informal working norm rather than a formal requirement, but it supports the formal strategy of rapid turn-around times to drive down costs.

Dynamic routines that are constantly improved upon. And the improvements stem from suggestions from frontline employees as well as managers and leaders. The formal processes are consistently followed because they are supplemented and supported by informal networks. As people experiment informally, the best improvements are then standardized into the formal processes in a regular rhythm. Toyota is the classic example, with its production line employees who are energized to constantly suggest and make quality improvements to the company's legendary, highly detailed vehicle assembly processes.

Work groups that grow organically to supplement and work across defined structures, yet maintain sufficient structure to execute efficiently. These groupings take advantage of common networks and often pave the way for more formal pathways. In the more savvy organizations, such pathways are frequently introduced only after informal trails have developed. For instance, Google has been very careful about not formalizing anything—such as a new product team, a development process, or a testing protocol—"too soon." Rather, the company encourages informal "grouplets" to pursue initiatives in their own ways, so long as they don't require significant resources or get in the way of other established working approaches.

A range of value propositions to satisfy employees with different goals and ambitions. For example, the high-potential A player is more focused on personal compensation and the advancement track, so annual promotions and salary increases dominate the value proposition. The quality-of-life B player is more focused on how people progress and work together productively, so daily and weekly accomplishments and peer recognition dominate the value proposition. The original Home Depot under founders Bernie Marcus and Arthur Blank was a great example of a place that created a strong sense of ownership, peer-to-peer reinforcements, and individual responsibility among employees.

Employees who are proud of the company, their colleagues, and their day-to-day accomplishments. Peer-based respect—and discipline at all levels—is at least as important as respect for the top leadership. The U.S. Marine Corps has developed a culture that integrates both formal and informal elements in ways that encourage pride and informal peer "disciplining" across all of its tiers.

An ecosystem of outside partners, suppliers, and customers who are motivated to help the organization succeed. For instance, the early adopters of Apple's Mac are avid followers of the company's every move. They want Apple to stay true to what they believe was its original intent to be the ultimate user-friendly computer. They are almost obsessive about attending every Apple convention or conference, and commenting on whatever concerns or intrigues them. Not surprisingly, the company wisely pays attention to their counsel. It creates formal platforms and forums in which to direct their informal passion.

These are a few indicators of integration that can't be easily deconstructed into either their formal or informal components. At a high level, it's hard to find the line that separates what's being mobilized informally and what's being managed formally. The two become fundamentally intertwined.

HOW THE INFORMAL WORKED FOR THE HOUSTON POLICE DEPARTMENT

Prime-time TV watchers know all about cops. For over a decade now the original *Law & Order* and its numerous offshoots have taken viewers into the nitty-gritty of police work. In a nutshell, we know that cops work two-person detective teams, with an occasional assist from a wise but demanding chief and the psychiatric criminologist. We also know that the "internal affairs" officers are really the bad guys, always trying to pin the blame on the really good detectives for some infraction or other.

As exciting as these tales may be, they don't tell us much about the formal and informal aspects of metropolitan police work. An awful lot of it is just persistent, routine, hard work that doesn't smack of TV heroism. In fact, it turns out that the most important factor in top-performing police departments is how effectively they integrate the formal and informal elements of their organization.

For example, organizational performance (defined as preventing crime as well as catching crooks) means a lot to the Houston Police Department (HPD). And this is a story of how the HPD increased performance by creating a new formal mechanism—the proactive policing group—to balance what the informal was already doing and thereby getting the best from both.

How well the police fulfill their mission has enormous consequences for the community since cutting crime is a high-stakes game. Officers and investigators consistently have to rely on one another to solve crimes and apprehend criminals. Not surprisingly, it turns out that the way they organize themselves to do so—both formally and informally—makes a big difference to their productivity and efficiency.

Like most police departments, Houston's is composed of two sets of officers: *Patrol,* which includes the officers who respond to emergency calls and are assigned to neighborhood-based precincts; and *Investigation,* composed of officers who are divided into crime-specific divisions like homicide and robbery. For the most part, the two sides of the force operate separately, but there are times when units from both sides have to interact.

At the Houston Police Department, responding to emergency calls is a necessary but time-consuming part of the job. Although emergency 911 calls are both high-profile and frequent, they do not produce a proportionate number of arrests. Thus they have little direct impact on reducing crime. In addition, they can distract patrol officers from conducting more specific, proactive police work beyond normal traffic citations or code violations.

Mike Faulhaber, a Houston sergeant, was convinced the department needed to focus more on preventing crimes—rather than on stopping them as they occurred. To Faulhaber, this meant creating more proactive (rather than reactive) policing behavior. But he also saw the need for a system that would accelerate response to emergency calls, while still allowing some officers to police more proactively.

Faulhaber also knew that another HPD sergeant had previously attempted to initiate a program similar to what he had in mind.

Unfortunately, that effort failed, sparking tremendous animosity across the squad. Simply put, the problem was cultivating a team of officers who were already proactively policing, while everyone else was left out of the loop. Anyone not on this chosen team was forced to pick up the slack of emergency calls. Not surprisingly, those left out resented the extra, less glamorous work. And, as a result, informal peer-to-peer interactions became increasingly counterproductive. It was a classic example of introducing a formal mechanism (the new squad, and by extension the left out squad) that rubbed against the grain of the existing informal mechanisms (that is, pride in more glamorous work).

So Faulhaber took a different approach based on self-selection. He established a new proactive policing group, set clear expectations for it, and gave everyone in the department the opportunity to sign up. Doing so would obviously mean more work for the volunteers, but it would also give them freedom from the interruption of emergency calls. Those officers who didn't sign up for the proactive group knew explicitly that they were expected to field 911 calls and pick up the slack.

Since the communication to the entire group defined the options and responsibilities very clearly, those who opted not to join the proactive patrol force did not feel that they were overlooked or unfairly overburdened. This simple mechanism of self-selection enabled people to align formal work routines with informal sources of motivation. An additional benefit was that the process seemed fair and was supported rather than resisted informally. The result was the integration of the formal and informal that would have been hard to reach with just one or the other.

The solution was a big success. The division sergeants are able to help plan and coordinate their projects, while giving the officers the autonomy to lead. In addition, the proactive officers receive excellent tactical, investigative, and problem-solving experience that

they would not necessarily receive otherwise and that is very benefi-
cial if they want to move up to a detective role.

Faulhaber energized the team by creating a dedicated group.
Note how his actions were guided by an awareness of the broader
informal organization, namely people's sense of pride as well as the
importance of peer support, and he introduced a formal mechanism
to capitalize on both. A true integration.

As is often the case, this mobilization of the informal organization had additional, unintended, and positive effects. The proactive
policing group has far-reaching effects on the informal organization.
Specifically, it helps Patrol officers strengthen their networks with
Investigation. Since that group spends a lot of time trying to solve
the problems that proactive policing is meant to help solve as well,
and since the officers in the new group have time dedicated to work
on a particular problem or crime, members of both groups are better
able to connect and work effectively together.

These new network connections are essential to the HPD on
both an immediate and long-term basis. For example, Investigation
officers often need immediate support from Patrol officers on the
ground. As Sergeant Zalud, an investigator in the Narcotics division,
explains, "Narcotics officers usually work undercover or in plain
clothes. We often have to rely on Patrol officers in uniform. That
gives the plainclothes officers some legitimacy when they're doing
street-level busts."

The Patrol officers best suited for this job are those who have
specialized knowledge about the neighborhoods where they work.
Collaborating with a Patrol officer who does not have the necessary
local knowledge can have dire consequences. Thus knowing which
officers are more interested in working with Investigations not only
makes the interactions easier and more successful, it also makes
them safer and more efficient.

In the old days, officers relied on their intuition to make the
choice. Now they know that those who volunteer for this new group

are truly invested in the process. And in the long run, Investigation relies on the strength of the Patrol ranks for most of its recruiting of talent. The proactive policing program not only identifies talent early, it also gives Patrol officers with an interest in investigations the training and skills that will bring them success if they decide to apply for positions on the other side of the department.

•　•　•　•　•　•　•　•　•

It's important to note the *way* Sergeant Faulhaber went about mobilizing, because the *how* is at least as important as what he actually did. Faulhaber created a formal group, but he did it in a way that allowed it to integrate with and be supported by (rather than aggravate) the informal organization. "We're all on the same team," he says. "Everyone in the department is working to arrest the same guy and make the city safer. That's our mission. We have to work together to do it." And his well-executed program, based solidly in existing informal tendencies, made it a whole lot easier to do so.

This is not as easy as it sounds. In any organization, the formal practitioners love the control, efficiency, and scale advantages that their personal favorite approach delivers. They can easily rationalize why process rigor, metric clarity, and analytic discipline will "sooner or later, make folks do what we want them to do." Unfortunately, they can also lose a lot of good workers and customers along the way.

Conversely, disciples of the informal can quote chapter and verse about the intangible benefits of empowerment, engagement, and emotional energy. Unfortunately, they can waste a lot of time and resources in the process of getting from A to B. That is why great organizations, great leaders, and great contributors invariably pay close attention to both dimensions of their organization.

PART TWO

MOTIVATING INDIVIDUAL PERFORMANCE

Most employees are less motivated by money than by how they feel about the work itself. While money attracts and retains talent, it's the pride people take in their daily or weekly accomplishments that invariably provides the motivation that drives top-quality work. Managers who can make the majority of their people feel good about the majority of their work achieve an advantage over managers who rely on formal rewards that only apply to a select few.

An important source of pride can be found in meaningful values, which are easier to state than to inculcate in behavior. Like most abstract sources of pride, high-sounding values need to be directly connected to the work itself, not just to institutional aspirations. And, most important, they need to focus people's attention on personal as well as business results. When this happens, the informal organization can generate emotional commitment toward formal performance objectives—and that generates performance results well beyond what rational compliance can generate.

This kind of extra effort can be found in work environments like the Gentle Giant moving company. Unlike most other moving companies, when Gentle

Giant moves your belongings, some members of the crew will actually run to and from the truck just for the exercise. The company's story is captured in this section along with other examples—business and nonbusiness—that illustrate the emotional power of the informal, particularly as it contributes to high performance.

• • • • • • • • •

4

It's All About the Work

One day we were talking with about a dozen field technicians at Bell Canada about how their manager, Tony Kwok, made them feel about their work.

"What gives you the most satisfaction about your job?" Zia asked.

"Oh that's easy," said a young woman we'll call Heather. "I love it when I can fix what no one else can."

Everyone in the room reacted. Some laughed. Some looked puzzled.

"You guys seem a little surprised by what Heather said," Zia commented.

"Yeah, a little," said one of the other technicians. "But she must be talking about somebody else, because no one here makes mistakes."

More laughter.

Zia then asked the group, "Were you aware that Heather likes fixing what other people can't?" There was a general shaking of heads in response to the question. Zia then asked Heather if Tony was aware of her source of job satisfaction?

"Of course he's aware," she said.

"How do you know that?" Zia asked.

"Because that's the only kind of assignment he gives me. And the more messed up, the better."

WHY PRIDE MATTERS MORE THAN MONEY— EVEN MORE THAN WE THOUGHT

Feeling good about day-to-day accomplishments is a strong source of motivation that influences behaviors. Unfortunately a lot of most people's daily work can be pretty boring, if not downright tedious and stressful, so "feeling good" about it is not as easy as it sounds. Moreover, those positive feelings come mostly from the informal organization.

One of the strongest positive emotional drivers is pride. Kids work harder in school for the teacher who makes them feel proud of getting a good grade or developing a new skill. Multimillionaire athletes stretch themselves to the limit for the pride of winning the championship—but also take pride in the rigorous training it requires. Pride in the journey can be as motivating as pride in the destination. Refinery workers will take extra care in their work for the pride of a clean safety record, or more simply the good feeling of helping a colleague avoid an injury.

Yet most motivational programs focus entirely on the formal rewards: money, perks, and promotions. Our research and experience show that how people feel about their work, and the pride they take in their daily or weekly accomplishments, can be a powerful motivator of their daily behavior. In research for *Why Pride Matters More Than Money*, and in work with clients afterwards, Katz developed the following insights about pride as a motivational force.[1]

What Matters Most Is How People Feel About What They Do

Pride is at the heart of what motivates peak performers in most human endeavors. This is evident in art, music, athletics, medicine, or popular entertainment. What motivated George Carlin to toil for many decades in comedy clubs was not the money or the recognition—it was the work itself, including the relentless preparation that characterized his appearances. What motivated Lance Armstrong to push himself to seven Tour de France victories was not the glory but the personal highs of training hard year in and year out. Our own field work confirms the inherent human need to feel good about what we do and how we do it, as does the academic work of thought leaders such as Abraham Maslow, Douglas McGregor, Peter Senge, and Frederic Herzberg.

Pride Has a Dark Side to Its Motivational Pull

The Old Testament calls pride the seventh deadly sin, and, we'd have to agree that pridefulness that is self-aggrandizing seldom motivates work that is in the long-term interest of the company. Of course, many people take pride in material things like yachts, mansions, and designer fashion. Companies that rely too much on monetary and material rewards for motivation invariably lose their best people to the highest bidders.

Pride, unfortunately, can motivate good and bad outcomes. A classic example of this was reported recently in Bob Sutton's blog "Work Matters."[2] It was from a piece of research Gary Latham conducted in a large sawmill where employees were stealing about $1 million in equipment every year. Because of the strong union it was virtually impossible to impose discipline on the offenders. However, Latham's research determined that much of what was being stolen was actually things the workers neither needed nor used; they were doing it for the thrill of it and to brag to their buddies, which they took great pride in doing.

Working with management, Latham came up with a system to "kill the thrill" by simply making the equipment available to all for personal use through a library system. Thus it was no longer fun or a source of pride to steal what could be otherwise obtained with management's permission. Once it no longer earned prestige in the peer culture, theft dropped to virtually zero—and the workers actually started returning all the stuff they had stolen earlier.

Good pride works the same way. Motivation through pride in the work and pride in the people you work with is a differentiated incentive, ideally one that is unique to the organization. That is why the informal elements of motivation are so important to understand and utilize. The key is to align and connect the pride people take in their work with positive performance outcomes.

Pride in the Journey Is as Important as Pride in the Destination

The best motivators have learned how to get their people to anticipate how good they will feel during the journey as well as at the end. The good manager will focus recognition on meeting or beating your monthly targets; managers that we call "master motivators," however, will go further and focus at least as much attention on recognizing the little things you have to do each day that will get you to and beyond the destination target. And the master motivator will also find ways to keep you feeling good about the hard work and effort you put forth even when you miss a monthly target.

Money, Perks, and Promotions Also Motivate People

The tangible elements of job rewards are important in meeting the survival and life-sustaining needs in Abraham Maslow's hierarchy. Most people place the highest priority on simply taking good care of their families. Once these fundamental needs are met, however, money becomes more important in attracting and retaining talent than it is in motivating behavior change and discretionary performance efforts.

Since Katz's work around *Why Pride Matters More Than Money*, four other concepts have come to light in the course of our work.

Feelings About the Company Motivate Loyalty Rather Than Behavioral Change

Pride in the company, and in its leaders, brands, and aspirations, is important in attracting and retaining talent. Motivating behavior change, however, is much more dependent on how a person feels about the work itself. While our original research identified work as one source of pride, it did not specify how it differs from other sources in changing work behaviors.

Any Organization Contains Multiple Sources of Pride

Successful motivators have learned through trial and error how to draw on different sources of pride for different people and purposes. For example, a company's mission, the quality of its products, or its role in sponsoring local sports teams are potential sources of pride. The key is to use those sources of pride in different ways to make emotional connections to each person's day-to-day work. For senior leaders this means ensuring a healthy flow of credible and diverse sources of pride to help give managers many options for creating pride. However, there is no substitute for an immediate supervisor who can make a variety of personal informal connections to instill pride in different individual work situations.

People Rarely Feel Pride in Isolation

There is almost always a real or imagined "pride audience" with whom individuals want to share their good feelings. The master motivators at all levels are keenly aware of, and learn to draw upon, those potential pride audiences. Parents and peers serve as that audience for many young people starting their careers, then their own families and a growing set of mentors join it. Sometimes former teachers, coaches, and role models can be a "resurfaced audience." For more experienced workers, the pride audience may be the individual's day-to-day colleagues. The sawmill example cited earlier showed how powerful this audience can be—even when the behavior is illegal.

People derive strong feelings of pride by reflecting on how their pride audience recognizes (or would recognize) an accomplishment. That is why the wise pride-builder will often send a personal note to the individual's home instead of relying on an impersonal card or quick and easy e-mail. They send handwritten personal notes for all sorts of reasons—not just formal events. And when they do use e-mail, it is thoughtfully crafted and copied to relevant peer and supervisory audiences. This also highlights the roles of networks and communities in driving pride in the day-to-day work.

Formal Rewards Can Sometimes Diminish Pride

While it's easy to see that rewards and pride motivate in different ways, something unexpected happens when both come into play in the same situation. Considerable study has been devoted to the combined effects of *extrinsic* motivators such as monetary rewards, and *intrinsic* motivators such as pride in the work. Do they combine in an additive fashion to create double motivation? In most cases, the answer is no.

It turns out that extrinsic rewards can actually reduce intrinsic motivation. Researchers have shown that when individuals have both sufficient extrinsic and intrinsic reasons for an activity, that activity is "overjustified," and people discount the intrinsic reason and overemphasize the extrinsic reason. It's a form of the cognitive dissonance reduction that Leon Festinger clarified in 1957.[3]

For example, when nursery school children are offered a "good player" award for drawing a picture, which they normally do happily, they are much less likely to do so spontaneously than their peers who are not offered this kind of extrinsic reward. Thus it's likely that money can sometimes undermine the natural pride that people take in their work. This is an important counterintuitive idea in a world that is largely driven by financial rewards. If you suddenly get paid to do something that was once a hobby, it can become a lot less like fun and more like a chore.

We also find that organizations that focus primary attention on rewarding people through significant monetary distinctions (such as investment banks and contract sales organizations) create a self-fulfilling prophecy. Because the formal reward system is mostly about money, people take pride in the size of their bonus and the material things they can afford to buy to show what they earn. This can easily override any informal efforts to instill pride in the work itself. A number of related studies show that when people are motivated by extrinsic rather than intrinsic rewards, the quality and creativity of their performance goes down.

Such studies do have their limitations. Nursery school, for example, is a very different place from the messy and complicated world of large organizations, but there is enough evidence to support the contention that when it comes down to lasting behavior change pride matters more than money. Moreover, in some cases, money can reduce pride and therefore lower intrinsic motivation. The result is that self-serving short-term efforts are emphasized at the expense of long-term performance. How many times have all of us talked about some aspect of our jobs and said, "Well, it puts food on the table"?[4] And how many career counselors start by asking their advisees what they would do if money wasn't the primary object?

THE CHARACTERISTICS OF PRIDE-BUILDERS

Pride-builders (or, alternatively, master motivators) have a great understanding of the importance of pride, are aware of the sources of pride both inside and outside their company, and are highly attuned to what instills pride in the individuals they work with.

Leaders who pay attention to master motivators invariably discover that they can be an incredible source of both insight and energy. Of course, master motivators help build pride in the work because they have generally learned how to make people feel good about the work they have to do. But they also know what elements of the organization are motivational inhibitors. On one hand, they epitomize behaviors that are typically overlooked or hidden within the comprehensive formal leadership model. They focus relentlessly on finding ways to instill pride in the work itself. This enables them to concentrate their efforts on enabling their people to strive to do their personal best. In other words, they deliver results by motivating their people intrinsically, rather than simply relying on rules of behavior, monetary rewards, and mastery of process.

However, contrary to the popular image of the people-people manager who tries to make the work environment fun, master motivators focus on results and hold their teams to high standards. In essence, they reject the false trade-off between making people feel good about their work and delivering results—they do both.

When it comes to motivating and pride-building, we identify three types of managers (compared in the following exhibit). The manager who would traditionally be considered "good" is the one who gets performance results largely by mastery of process and metrics. The "people person" tries to create a social and happy environment. These are the managers who tend to favor superficial perks, such as popcorn makers and Friday afternoon massages. And then there are the pride-builders.

One of the major reasons that "good" managers have trouble motivating frontline staff is that they think of the front line as a homogeneous mass, rather than as a collection of unique individuals and informal relationships. Therefore they believe that applying formal mechanisms such as performance incentives consistently across the board is the best way to motivate the workforce. This also allows

Contrasting Categories of Managers

	A "Good" Manager	A "People Person"	A "Pride-Builder"
Is Passionate About . . .	Measurable results	Personal feelings Being well liked Having fun	Connecting company needs to each individual's definition of success Getting each person to strive for a "personal best"
Makes Decisions by . . .	Being fair and rational; focusing on efficiency and measurable impact of decisions; treating all equally	Talking through issues with their team; explaining "the why" while remaining hands-on; becoming personally popular	Actively involving staff in finding solutions; empowering people to pursue ideas even if not in full agreement Getting the best of conflicting ideas
Develops People by . . .	Helping only those with higher potential progress along formal development paths Focusing on formal monetary and advancement rewards	Using their contacts to create development opportunities for personal favorites	Acting as a powerful agent for people's holistic development Role-modeling expected behaviors Settling for nothing less than a "personal best" effort from each person
May Be Described as . . .	"A really good manager—I'm confident with Sam at the helm" "Gives me the tools to get the job done"	"Easy to work with—believes people matter more than numbers" "I really like Sam" Someone who likes to be liked	"Someone you never want to disappoint" "Sam trusts me in ways that make me a better person as well as a better worker—makes me want to go above and beyond" "Not easy to work for, but always really energizing"

them to leverage their time most efficiently because they don't have to waste time worrying about individual differences.

Of course, it is not possible for even the most accomplished pride-builder to motivate every person on the front line in a completely individualized way. Yet treating everyone the same way overlooks the diversity of aspirations and definitions of success that are at the heart of highly motivated individuals. We believe the key to energizing individual behavior in an orderly way is to mobilize the informal organization to create a tailored and personal motivating experience—one that complements and balances the formal mechanisms that help ensure consistent and efficient behavior across large numbers of people.

An Unexpected Motivator: Lessons from the World of Politics

A brief word of warning: those who cannot abide politics or who have particularly strong feelings about the 2004 presidential election may take issue with this section. We are about to sing the praises of a (former) Republican political operative, Kenneth B. Mehlman. Our interest in Mehlman's experience is not tied to either our or his political opinions but to show how an insightful public sector executive found ways to balance the informal and formal elements of his organization in the context of a very high-stakes and challenging situation.

As we see it, whatever his politics, Kenneth B. Mehlman is a master motivator. And political leaders from both parties who have known Mehlman have been equally vocal and positive about his capabilities.

When Mehlman took over the 2004 campaign to re-elect President George W. Bush, he knew he was facing an uphill battle. All political campaigns can be torturous management conundrums in which vindictive politics, super-sized egos, and personal ambitions abound. The mother of all campaigns, and therefore the most complex of these conundrums, is the U.S. presidential election.

Presidential campaign managers, for both parties, are in effect leaders of multimillion-dollar organizations that come into existence very rapidly, run through their entire funding in eighteen months, and are then almost completely dismantled. A successful political campaign has to be responsive to unexpected change almost daily. This is an extreme leadership, management, and organizational challenge.

Even tougher, with Bush's approval rating below 50 percent, history was against Mehlman and his team. The best predictor of success in midterm elections is the incumbent's approval rate, and no incumbent in modern elections had ever won the midterm election with a rating below 50 percent. As Mehlman reminded us, "The President was in a very difficult situation when the election came around."

Despite this inauspicious beginning, Bush managed to get 51 percent of the vote and as we all know, he won. One of the reasons behind this win (of course not the only one, as Mehlman points out) was the campaign's ability to mobilize the emotional aspects of his informal campaign organization and instill in his people an incredible sense of pride in their work.

Mehlman's rise to the top in the world of political campaigns came about from his almost doggedly driven personality and philosophy of integrating the informal with the formal elements of leadership and organization. He describes himself as a hard-core, strategic numbers guy who is more interested in people's performance than their management of relationships. His discipline carries into his personal life as well; he works out for an hour and a half every day and sleeps six or seven hours each night. He firmly believes that, as he puts it, "You will make time for what you really want to do."

So, although "being nice" isn't something Mehlman worries much about, he is savvy enough to understand the importance of the informal organization. In the grueling world of campaigns, an emotionally committed workforce isn't a nice-to-have, it's a must-have.

Mehlman's awareness of how pride motivates people has roots in his childhood. When he was a boy, his father once explained that doormen in New York take great pride in their work because they feel they are part of the greatest, most important city in the world—an observation that resonated with the young Ken, and still remains a factor in his work.

He developed an intuitive understanding of the pride-builder concepts. Later in life, he became a strong advocate of giving the right jobs to the right people, setting up teams that balanced everyone's best strengths, and spontaneously recognizing hard work in ways that get people feeling good about it.

Making the Fact Checkers Take Pride in Their Work

Political campaigns are exciting, but the day-to-day work can be long, hard, and tedious. It can be challenging to keep people fully energized to perform their individual best at tasks that seem far-removed from the overall mission. Few tasks are more mundane than fact-checking; yet getting the facts wrong can put a candidate under harrowing media glare.

In the White House, there was a department that vets all documents before the president sees them. But the 2000 campaign had no such function, and documents were often hastily written and filled with errors. So, early in the 2004 campaign, Ken Mehlman brought on three people to proof and vet all formal documents to make sure they were what he called "White House ready." This looked like busy-work to outsiders, but actually required a lot of thought and attention to detail. So Mehlman set up the document-checkers in an office right next to his own. Basically, he believed their prominent position would help them take pride in their unglamorous work and would also force their fellow campaign workers to see them in a more positive light. Mehlman made a point of expressing his appreciation frequently, spontaneously, and in ways that were visible to colleagues.

Tapping the potential of everyone on a team, no matter what their role, requires appreciating them and making sure they feel good about the work they have to do. By giving the fact-checkers a place of prominence (and in scores of other such actions), Mehlman regularly conveyed to his entire team a powerful motivating message—often without actually having to say it: "We're all part of something very special here; no matter what you do, it matters."

Giving Respect If You Expect to Get It

Right or wrong, Mehlman believed that Republicans were traditionally not as good as Democrats at establishing and maintaining relationships with the media. Whatever the reason—habitual grudges, ideological differences, personal styles—he saw Republicans struggle to capitalize on their media relationships. "It's a self-compounding dynamic that has made Republicans wary of the press, and the media distrustful of Republicans," he says.

He set out to change this dynamic. Mehlman and his communications team put together a three-part plan. First, they would reach out regularly and directly to reporters. Second, they would be respectfully open, up-front, and proactive in giving them opportunities to ask questions and to examine policy ideas. And third, they would find ways for press people to personally familiarize themselves with campaign staff.

The challenge of part three was to find ways to get reporters and campaign staffers to feel good about interactions that would build mutual respect. "They may not always write nice things about your candidate," Mehlman says, "but if they're treated well, they're more likely to at least remain unbiased." He knew that if his staff showed the press the proper respect, reporters would be likely to reciprocate. He also used this as yet another source of pride to motivate his team.

Bestowing Power on Others

Like most political campaign managers, Ken Mehlman wanted formal control of all spending and hiring. Unlike most, however, he was determined to use his official base of control in an aggressive but informal way to create commitment and energize initiative. He bestowed much of the power to decide and act quickly on others, and thereby gained their full support while minimizing the risk of conflicting messages. He knew they would be proud of their ability to do so.

Mehlman had worked in the 2000 election campaign as a field manager, a job that that gave him valuable insight into the needs of campaign workers at all levels and in all geographies. This experience convinced him that control at the top often meant little consideration for specific needs on the ground. When it was his turn to run the show in 2004, he created a preliminary budget for the entire campaign. Then he went to the regional heads and worked with them to refine and adjust the plan to better fit the needs of each area. "I told my regional directors that this wasn't going to be top-down management," he told us. "I have a budget, but it is certainly wrong, since it is based on the past. Tell me what will work for the future."

As the campaign progressed, he met monthly with his business unit heads to review performance and to make further adjustments. As a result, the division leaders felt real ownership over their budgets, so they cared about saving money and not exceeding their limits. They were proud that he trusted them to run their own budgets. Simple, but rare. His fundamental premise was that in situations of unexpected, rapid change, "the top leader has to *be able to be led* from the bottom."

Mehlman took a similar approach to metrics. He was rigorous, if not fanatical, about developing performance metrics for virtually anything and everything. For example, he tracked the number of new voters registered per state and worked with the regional teams to set a target number. Because the state teams were invested in the creation of the metrics, they were also invested in meeting and exceeding them. This emotional involvement allowed his leadership team to introduce more metrics, giving them even more knowledge of various aspects of performance, and energized his team to work toward creating a greater performance advantage. "When the middle of your organization is actively involved in shaping the metrics, they also feel ownership of the metrics you introduce together. Consequently they don't feel that metrics represent oppression from the top down." Interestingly, they take pride in both shaping and meeting the metrics.

• • • • • • • • •

Motivating (or at least influencing the behaviors of) coworkers is a task that all of us face sooner or later. While most of the motivation challenge in large organizations is considered a formal "top-down" matter, the more admirable enterprises take advantage of three motivational vectors: top down, bottom up, and peer to peer.

Perhaps the most overlooked opportunity today lies within the peer-to-peer arena. Peer respect is a powerful source of pride, and hence motivation, particularly when it is based on the mutual respect that stems from a real working relationship. Motivational leaders invariably treat their subordinates as peers as often as they can.

Clearly, peer respect of an individual's work and performance is a major source of motivation. And it is a critical characteristic of highly committed organizations like IDEO, Microsoft, and the Navy Seals. While hierarchies exist in these situations, and while they are a very important element for realizing performance imperatives, the power of peer respect is equally apparent. In our work and research, we seldom encounter peak-performing organizations or groups that do not capitalize on peer-to-peer interactions in sustaining strong feelings of pride in the work itself.

5

Values Driven,
Not Values Displayed

onsider two well-known organizations whose stated values were similar. Organization A had *communication, respect, integrity,* and *excellence.* These values were posted on the company Web site, included in the employee manual, and printed on wallet cards distributed at company events. However, looking at the company's employee engagement survey results, we found a large and disturbing gap in the degree to which people actually subscribed to these values. They didn't necessarily disagree with them—who could disagree with any of those four words?—they just didn't *apply* them to determine their decisions and behavior.

The values of Organization B were *honor, courage,* and *commitment.* These words are a little more unusual than those of Organization A, perhaps, but still nothing particularly exceptional. The real difference in these words is how the values actually determine critical behavior. Every person in this organization talks openly about the values, and makes critical, even life-saving decisions, based on them.

Can you guess the two organizations?

Organization A was Enron. As we all know, it went bankrupt after massive accounting irregularities came to light in 2001. Enron's

CEO, Jeff Skilling, is in jail—and his lawyers are still in court arguing his appeal.

Organization B is the U.S. Marine Corps (USMC). It has endured for more than two hundred years as an elite, high-performing institution—winning our nation's most difficult battles time and again.

A critical difference between these organizations lies in the use of the informal organization to bring the values to life. Enron was a values-*displayed* organization, where the values were nothing more than words on paper, cited in speeches and presentations when convenient. The Marine Corps is a values-*driven* organization, in which the values are lived, breathed, and drawn upon to guide day-to-day actions and decisions.

VALUES AS ORGANIZATIONAL GUIDES

Values are beliefs about what's important and what kinds of behaviors reflect that importance. Since companies cannot—and should not—dictate every move an employee makes, values can serve as the North Star that guides actions and decisions. They come to life through the actions of leaders, and leading people to make the right choices when no one else is around.

At McKinsey & Company, for example, it has been common for senior directors to ask themselves in difficult situations, "What would Marvin do?" Marvin Bower was the firm's legendary founder, who died in 2003. His values of professionalism and excellent client service plus the way he demonstrated and lived them every day continue to exert influence—not only at McKinsey, but throughout the consulting profession.

Values are both formal and informal. They are formal in that they can be written down, displayed throughout an organization's physical space, and fleshed out in elaborate memoranda. They emanate from on high and are disseminated through the hierarchy. However, it's the informal organization that is responsible for elevating values from admirable statements to a way of life. In a values-driven organization, the values are shared and promoted not just through formal means but by people who act consistently and communicate constantly, simultaneously "walking the talk" and "talking the walk." They are espoused and enforced among peers as well as by superiors at all levels. Values help organizations outperform their competitors, and success further reinforces the values. Not surprisingly, very few organizations can legitimately claim to be truly values driven.

We all know one or more of the more famous values-driven organizations, be it the Marines, Southwest Airlines, or Johnson & Johnson with its famous credo. But perhaps the following relatively unknown example will better illustrate the challenge and the potential.

GENTLE GIANT: VALUES-DRIVEN CUSTOMER SERVICE

Driving long distances, lifting heavy boxes, and moving bulky furniture in and out of oddly configured homes is not glamorous work. It involves sweat, muscle strain, and repetitive tasks. Even so, the employees at Gentle Giant, a moving company with sixteen regional branches throughout New England, love their jobs. Gentle Giant's workers load and unload boxes and trucks with surprising vigor and enthusiasm. In an industry notorious for high turnover and poor customer service, Gentle Giant has attracted dedicated, capable employees and kept them productively engaged—largely because most people in the company truly strive to live its values every day.

When we met Gentle Giant's CEO, Larry O'Toole, we were immediately struck by his sheer size. An easy-mannered former Harvard crew rower who grew up on a farm in Ireland, he towered over us. Yet his hulking frame matched the height of his giant employees.

Larry started Gentle Giant because he saw a strong need for quality customer service in the moving business. He had begun his post-Harvard life as an engineer in a large company. Unsatisfied, he dreamed of starting his own business. He quit his job and worked for a moving company to pay the rent, while he figured out what kind of company to start. He found that he enjoyed the physical nature of the work, because it reminded him of his childhood spent on a farm. He also discovered that people liked the way he moved their belongings. While most movers can be careless and slow, Larry was attentive, genial, and fast.

Early on, Larry recognized that he could offer a kind of moving service that no other company provided. So he placed a $17 ad in a Boston newspaper, and people responded. At the outset, he did the moving himself with just one small truck.

Today, the company is thriving and expanding rapidly along the Eastern seaboard. Gentle Giant has won many awards from the Better Business Bureau, *Boston Magazine,* and the Greater Boston Chamber of Commerce. The company was recognized in 2007 by the *Wall Street Journal* for being one of the top ten small workplaces.

Connect Values to the Work

You are very unlikely to find Gentle Giant's combination of values in any other company—"skilled athleticism," "teamwork," and "personal customer caring." Larry knows that values that are relevant to the challenges of the work itself will drive performance and these three not only set the company apart from its many competitors but are also integral to the moving of household effects. They are also integral to what attracts, motivates, and resonates with prospective employees who will excel in the job.

Larry places particular emphasis on the value of athleticism (particularly upper-body strength) for a fairly obvious reason. Moving is strenuous work and doing it well requires movers to be in good physical condition. When the company started in the moving business more than twenty-five years ago, Larry recruited athletes. He refused to accept the stereotype of a mover: the big lug who takes long smoke breaks and lumbers up and down stairs. No, Larry wanted athletes like rowers, with lots of upper body strength and plenty of stamina. Even today, many of Gentle Giant's movers and office staff are former rowers and the terminology at Gentle Giant revolves around rowing metaphors. The crews at Gentle Giant, for example, pile boxes into "the boats" rather than trucks.

New hires at Gentle Giant are given extensive training anchored by a deep-seated company tradition: every new hire has to run up and down the thirty-seven sets of 120 steps in Harvard Stadium. Thus Gentle Giant's values of athleticism and teamwork are tangible and, because everyone has to go through the ritual, the stadium climbing brings the company together in a memorable shared experience. Larry himself still joins in the step-climbing exercise as often as he can.

Stadium running is fun and builds relationships, but the athleticism it requires is fundamental to the work of moving furniture, as new employees learn through the training course, Gentle Giant 101. Once they start working, movers continue to train on a frequent basis, often on the job. They learn basic skills such as how to move a piano, as well as new techniques like the fine points of packing up china or getting an antique desk down a flight of rickety stairs. In fact, there are fifty specialized modules, and employees who complete them receive a stamp (like a Boy Scout merit badge) to paste into a "passport." These serve as a record of the employee's progress in training and skill building and are a tremendous source of pride.

Spread Your Values Through Stories

When Briain Coleman, the training director at Gentle Giant, first came to the United States from Ireland, he imagined his job at the company as a stepping stone to something bigger and better (although he wasn't quite sure what) but clearly not a career. Now he spends his days thinking about how to teach newcomers what makes Gentle Giant special. He believes only 10 percent of the job can be transferred through formal training. The other 90 percent has to be learned on the "boats."

Moving crews spend a lot time together, traveling from one house to another, and they spend much of their time telling stories to amuse each other, but also to teach. Briain knows this very well, and catalyzes the learning by mixing up the crews so that stories spread more quickly throughout the organization.

Briain told us about a crew that was struggling to move a large armoire into an apartment up five flights of narrow stairs. It seems that the crew successfully hefted the piece to the top of the fifth-floor stair, but could not get it into the hallway. After trying every maneuver they could think of, the crew chief finally reported the bad news to the customer, along with profuse and heartfelt apologies. The customer refused to accept that this was the end of the line. "Why do you think we hired Gentle Giant in the first place," he demanded. "I heard you're the best. So, if you're the best, you should be able to come up with something."

The chief huddled with his crew and they agreed that he should give Briain a call. He might be able to think of something. Briain said he would hurry right over. Just as he was leaving the office, another crew chief returned from a job and Briain told him what was going on. The second crew chief jumped in a truck with Briain, even though he knew he wouldn't get paid for the job.

Together, the crew came up with a solution. They took the armoire back down the stairs, rigged a hoist on the roof of the porch of the apartment, hauled it up, swung it onto the porch, and at last carried it into the bedroom of the fifth-floor apartment. The customers cheered, as did a group of onlookers that had gathered on the street below.

The story is legendary throughout the Gentle Giant organization and movers still tell it to each other—and to newcomers—constantly. Why? It illustrates perfectly and dramatically what the company is all about. People pitch in to do difficult physical tasks for customers because they care about their colleagues, the company's customers, and the company's reputation. No job can stump the movers at Gentle Giant!

Storytelling among colleagues and peers is one of the most natural and effective ways to spread values that drive behavior. A repertoire of stories that illustrate a particular values-based behavior helps teach how that value can be applied in a range of situations. The act of storytelling is also a very human and emotion-driven experience. Good stories spread far and wide, allowing people to "talk the walk" and take part in the narrative even if they had nothing to do with it themselves. And good stories always bear repeating.

Let Customers Reinforce Values

Because movers are in close contact with customers, they receive immediate feedback about how the values of the company are being lived. Since they are able to move furniture quickly and skillfully—during what is typically a very stressful and highly emotional event for most people—they see firsthand the impact of a job well done.

Gentle Giant movers believe so deeply in the importance of skilled athleticism that it is not at all uncommon to see them actually *run* back to the truck after they've completed a trip into the house with a box or piece of furniture. Why? What better way to speed up the moving process and keep fit at the same time? Needless to say, this display of enthusiasm and fitness deeply impresses customers and convinces them that they are in the hands of a *very* special breed of mover. The presence of the customers, and the pride the movers take in pleasing them, influences the movers' behavior as much as having a leader on-site giving them a pat on the back.

When a crew arrives on a job, it is common practice for each member of a moving team to introduce himself to each member of the family. Throughout the day, the crew members often offer to help customers do things that have nothing to do with the moving contract—like emptying the clothes dryer or carrying out the garbage.

As a result of the culture of athleticism (and the founder's zeal), the movers at Gentle Giant are dedicated to their customers and speedy with their work. Their shared values, sense of teamwork, storytelling, and pride in helping customers all reinforce each other consistently to influence daily actions. The company charges more than many of its rivals, but Larry tells us that most customers are convinced—usually within the first twenty minutes of the job—that Gentle Giant is well worth the premium.

How Reliant Survived: Bringing New Values to Life

In 2002, Reliant, an energy company based in Houston, found itself floundering in a sea of uncertainty. The Texas electricity market was being deregulated. New competitors seemed to be appearing every day. So the company needed to prepare for an unregulated marketplace *and* combat the wave of new competition. No longer could it prosper by playing the game of appeasing the regulators. Now it really had to compete for customers, which meant keeping costs as low as possible.

At the same time, the fall of its Houston corporate neighbor, Enron—also an energy company—caused a serious shock to the Reliant organization. When Enron was the darling of Wall Street, Reliant wanted to emulate it. When Enron collapsed in disgrace, Reliant wanted nothing more than to distance itself from anything "Enron-like."

Enron's downfall was so visibly disruptive it caused Reliant employees to question whether their company would suffer a similar fate. The prevailing mood throughout the company was one of despair. Many employees, as Karen Taylor, SVP of Human Resources, told us, "felt like they were on a sinking ship."

The challenges became even more dire when a credit crunch in 2002 threatened the company's financial stability. Reliant had recently acquired several power-generating facilities in New York state, leaving it with too little in liquid assets. As the credit crunch worsened, some of Reliant's loans were called, and management had to scramble to scrape together enough cash to make the payments. The share price, which had soared to above $30 after the company went public in May 2001, plunged to under $1 in October 2002. With few supporters in financial markets, little cash, and creditors screaming for payment, Reliant found itself near bankruptcy.

It seemed inconceivable that management could pull the company back from the brink of disaster, but they did. How? By mobilizing the informal to energize the formal.

Putting Values First

As a first move, Reliant's board of directors replaced the company's CEO in April 2003 with Joel Staff, who had served as a member of Reliant's board. Staff was chosen because of his extensive experience and stellar reputation as a turnaround expert.

The question was whether Reliant could be turned around by anyone. When Staff took the reins, Reliant had amassed $7.8 billion in debt, a lot for a company with annual revenue of $29 billion and assets totaling about $32 billion.[1] Of course, Staff would have to pull a bunch of formal levers—cost-cutting, headcount reduction, and streamlining processes—and fast. However, Staff and his management team knew that these top-down directives would only take them so far. Reliant would also have to find a way to reinvent itself.

Staff believed that creating a values-driven culture was the key to rallying the organization around the tough choices that had to be made and the substantive change that was sure to follow. He had faith that Reliant could fix itself by making values the primary determinant of behavior throughout the company while still being tough-minded and disciplined about its strategic and operational imperatives.

Soon after being named CEO, Staff assembled his senior leaders at an offsite to develop a plan of action and establish a set of values to guide them. As David Brast, SVP of Commercial Operations, told us, "Joel took us back to the basics. He challenged us to think of people in the company who were already manifesting the kinds of behaviors we wanted to encourage. By studying those 'behavioral exemplars,' we could better define and demonstrate the values we wanted to spread."

After much discussion and thought at the offsite, Staff and his senior leaders zeroed in on three fundamental values:

- Absolute integrity
- Collaboration, support, and respect
- Open, honest, and frequent communication

Obviously, there is nothing particularly magical about the words themselves. However, each of these values could be described and demonstrated in ways that most Reliant people instinctively believed, and that would appeal emotionally to leaders and employees alike. And that helped build confidence and credibility both within and outside of the organization.

Leaders Have to Walk the Talk

Staff told us that to reinvent the company, he knew he had to find ways to get the entire workforce living and demonstrating the core values through their decisions and actions every day—rather than simply dutifully mouthing the words. He had already started the process by selecting people for his senior leadership team who exemplified the values that he believed needed to permeate the company. He knew that they had to be demonstrated through decisions and action at the top if he expected the rest of the organization to behave accordingly.

Staff frequently assembled his team of senior leaders, who came from a broad range of backgrounds and experiences. He brought them together to encourage healthy discussion and share critical information about the company's progress. Increasingly, they worked together as a cohesive unit, often explicitly citing the values in their decision making. And they often told stories about employees taking action that demonstrated the values.

Because of the Enron legacy, the value of absolute integrity became particularly important at Reliant. To the company's leaders, *absolute* integrity meant communicating with sincerity and candor—no sugarcoating allowed. This value set Reliant well apart from Enron (which, perhaps ironically, shared the similar stated value of integrity), galvanized people to take pride in the company, and became a vital consideration in decision making.

The senior leadership team inculcated the values by communicating openly (both formally and informally) and honestly with their people at every opportunity. For example, Staff's team created a series of recurring Tuesday Talks, informal brown bag lunches that different leaders would hold with different groups of employees every week. People from across the organization could interact with a senior leader to gain a firsthand perspective on the current situation and get straightforward and honest answers to hard-hitting questions about the company's future.

Staff told us that the most common question at these events was, not surprisingly, some version of "Am I going to lose my job?" As part of the senior leadership's commitment to open and honest communication, the executive who was hosting the Tuesday Talk would not skirt the issue. Instead, he would say, "I can't guarantee your job or anyone else's for that matter, but I can assure you that the best way for us to keep as many jobs as possible is by pushing ourselves to work hard together."

The Tuesday Talks were extremely popular and effective, so much so that Reliant had to institute a lottery system to determine who would attend when. These events strengthened informal networks simply by bringing together employees who were deeply invested and concerned about Reliant's survival. For people battling feelings of confusion, insecurity, and uncertainty, the chance to ask difficult questions and get straight answers relieved a lot of anxiety and stress. Even though the number of people who could attend was relatively small, you can be sure that the participants spread the executives' answers far and wide—and with lightning speed through their informal networks and peer interactions.

Senior leaders were adamant about maintaining transparency in their other forms of communication as well. For example, Staff recorded weekly voicemail messages and sent them to all employees. These messages provided a report of the company's performance and often helped to dispel false rumors about what was going on and where the company was headed.

The Company Follows Suit

As Reliant's senior leaders opened the channels of communication, people throughout the ranks of the organization began to emulate their behavior. For example, Mike Kuznar, the director of Reliant's Customer Care group, held a series of Meals with Mike, modeled after the Tuesday Talks. The meals were open to any member of the customer service team. Mike fielded their tough questions and gave frank answers. For employees who were anxious about losing their jobs, this was an opportunity to learn about the company's performance at the local level. Mike helped them understand how their everyday work fit into the bigger picture of the company's challenges. In the end, Reliant survived. Its share price bounced back. The company retained most of its customers. And the informal organization grew stronger than ever.

In a turnaround like Reliant's, leaders are tempted to rely on formal mechanisms and measures. They want to cut costs, keep tight control, deliver messages and directives from the top. Reliant did all these things, but its leaders differ from their counterparts at other companies in that they complemented the necessary formal actions with a values-driven effort that bolstered important and visible behaviors throughout the informal organization and accelerated its recovery.

Unfortunately, Reliant's challenges did not end after the turnaround. As the company geared up for growth, it was struck by a perfect storm of external factors beyond anyone's control. In 2008, Hurricane Ike destroyed Galveston, one of Reliant's major markets. Later that year, the global credit crisis struck, wiping out critical financial support that Reliant needed in the wake of Ike. At last, in 2009, Reliant was bought by NRG Energy. None of this, however, negates the turnaround accomplishment that preceded it.

Ultimately, the company's recovery story is one of success. Its ability to survive the tremendous challenges it faced by using values as a driving force in the journey sets it apart from companies that espouse values but do not live them.

BIRDS OF A FEATHER: TRANSMITTING VALUES

People often seek out people who are like themselves. Having common values is part of what keeps groups together. Whereas timeliness may be seen as critical to one group; flexibility is critical to another. And people are attracted to groups that share their values, prejudices, and circumstances.

When we survey informal networks, we're able to ask respondents who they spend time with. We're also able to ask them to prioritize among a list of commonly held values. We often find that small communities within networks share similar values. For example, executives who prioritize "creativity" as a value are likely to have many connections among others who say the same, and to have fewer connections with executives who prize "no wasted time" as a value. This is a principle known as *homophily,* which means that we tend to associate and bond with those who are like us. This suggests an important interrelationship among the value mechanisms and the network mechanisms in the informal organization.

An article in the *New York Times* magazine described a phenomenon known as "social contagion"—the startling behavior changes that can happen among those in close social proximity to each other.[2] The author probes the dynamics behind the widely reported *New England Journal of Medicine* article by Nicholas Christakis and James Fowler that describes the finding that if your friend is obese, there is a 57 percent chance that you will become obese, as well.[3] More startling, there was a 20 percent chance of becoming obese if a friend of a friend became obese, even if the intermediate friend did not gain weight. The authors hypothesize that the behaviors spread because, subconsciously, we calibrate our sense of normalcy according to what we see others do.

This is an important phenomenon for managers to consider when thinking about how to change values in an organization. By focusing on observable behaviors that the company's values suggest, and encouraging the demonstration of those behaviors, managers can transmit these signals through networks and redefine what is normal. "Walking the talk" is important, particularly for senior leaders who transmit messages to a wider audience, and with a more powerful signal, than others in the organization do.

At times, shared values and the underlying network relationships can be difficult to detect. A story in the *Economist* highlights a surprising example of this in a firm called Cataphora, which specializes in e-discovery:[4] the mining of electronic records in the discovery phase of a lawsuit to "provide the clearest, most accurate insight into individual and organizational behavior based on the extensive trail of 'digital footprints' including email, text messages, documents, phone calls, and instant messages that we all create each day."[5]

In one example, Cataphora's solution detected an unusual sign-off phrase used by several executives at a firm that had been issuing fraudulent invoices. This phrase was associated with a college fraternity with which the executives were associated. This highlights the subtle webs of networks that we all belong to, and how they each may transmit different values to differing degrees. Recognizing these kinds of subwebs not only increases our understanding of how information travels, it also enables us to both use and shape them to advantage.

● ● ● ● ● ● ● ● ●

No organization will argue against the importance of values. But few recognize the benefit of using values to meaningfully energize employees and translate strategy into day-to-day expectations. Fewer still dedicate the leadership time to truly embed values into the broad-based organizational behaviors and decisions. Too often leaders believe that capturing an appealing set of words on a flip chart and then broadly communicating those words is sufficient. Unfortunately it is not, and the missed opportunity is substantial.

6

It's Still About Performance

When we introduce the idea of the informal organization to clients they often respond by saying something like, "You're talking about the soft stuff, right? Emotional intelligence? Feelings? Morale? Engagement?"

Yes. And no. The informal organization is indeed about feelings: pride, connection, resistance, fear, and accomplishment. But leading outside the lines is ultimately about influencing behaviors that determine performance and results. In fact, it is very often about *accelerating* results rather than ultimately eking them out!

Those of you who are sports fans know that coaches of championship efforts pay just as much attention to the emotional aspects of the game as they do to the skills involved. One without the other falls short in business too. Indeed, the informal organization is most successfully mobilized when there is also a sharp focus on performance. People want to know that their collaboration is leading to an improvement in results.

MAKING SOUP MATTER:
USING METRICS TO BUILD PRIDE AND PERFORMANCE

Ed Carolan knows a lot about making soup. He also is a master at using tailored performance objectives to motivate frontline workers. Ed is the general manager for StockPot, a subsidiary of The Campbell Soup Company that makes fresh refrigerated soup for the food service industry.

We first met Ed Carolan at the StockPot facility in Everett, Washington. We entered the sun-drenched lobby of the new large-volume plant, checked in at reception, and were told that he would join us in a moment. We waited, expecting that he would conform to our admittedly stereotypical image of a general manager of a manufacturing facility: clean-cut, uniformed, sober-sided, technically oriented. Then Carolan appeared, goatee, blue jeans, black motorcycle boots, and all. He bounded down the stairs, pumped our hands, and said, "Ready for a plant visit?" In a moment, we were off on a factory tour like none we had ever experienced—so detailed, so delightful, so colorful that we felt as if we were in a *Sesame Street* episode.

As we walked and talked, we learned that Carolan had become vice president and general manager of StockPot in January 2007. At the time, StockPot was in need of a turnaround. In the two years before Carolan arrived, profitability had dropped significantly, sales had declined for consecutive years, the subsidiary ranked near the bottom of the Campbell Global Supply Chain in safety and other key operational metrics, and employee engagement scores trailed the overall Campbell Soup Company.

But within two years of his arrival, Carolan and his team had achieved a turnaround. In his first year, profitability stabilized, and in the next—in the midst of a very bad recession—it shot up by 50 percent. One of the toughest metrics to improve in a down market is overall plant efficiency. Improvements were generally made in tenths of a percent, and even those require a lot of sweat and persistence. Under the new team, overall plant efficiency jumped 23 percent. Employee engagement scores increased by 14 percent. And, again in the midst of difficult times for everyone's wallets, the workers beat their United Way campaign goals and raised 27 percent more than the previous year. In fact, they won the United Way Community Partner Award for the top company making a difference in Snohomish County, while driving phenomenal performance improvements the whole time.

During our tour of the plant, the strong morale was palpable, as it was in our interviews with workers throughout the facility. People obviously felt a sense of pride and purpose in their work. The place surged with purposeful energy.

How did Carolan's team create such a remarkable transformation in such a short time? They focused on a limited number of measurable performance objectives. And they did so in a way that was personal, spontaneous, and full of, yes, positive feeling. Most important, they connected the two together.

Metrics Must Connect Strategy to Day-to-Day Work

Early on, Carolan's team recognized that in order to improve the company's performance they needed to drive more focus and resources toward large retailers. This would enable them to take advantage of their capacity to produce in large volumes and to cut down the number of stock-keeping units they produced for inventory, both important considerations in a business with considerable fixed costs.

As part of this effort, the team also needed to adjust the perception of StockPot. It was already viewed as a quality soup; now they wanted it to be thought of as a good eat-at-home meal.

It was a smart strategy—and a fortunate one, given the tough economic times. The pressure on people's wallets was driving them away from restaurants and into supermarkets looking for prepared foods to eat at home.

It was also a strategy that required some significant changes in the way StockPot did business. To focus on world-class grocery retailers would mean meeting their demands in terms of competitive costs, high quality, and great service.

One of the keys to driving the change was Carolan's focus on metrics that matter and motivate. To that end, he needed to make the organization more values-driven than it had been, and that required understanding how employees currently viewed the values. So Carolan and several members of his leadership team conducted a series of small group roundtable discussions that involved almost all of the 350 people in the plant. In the groups, he learned four things:

- People worked in routines they had followed for years.
- They had made little or no attempt to improve those routines.
- The company did not have a clear strategy.
- No one discussed performance results openly or even knew much about them.

And, as Carolan suspected, there was little commitment to the company's values, even though people could generally articulate what they thought the values were supposed to be. As a result, morale was low, collaboration was minimal, and teamwork was nonexistent.

Carolan and his team synthesized the input from the roundtable discussions, made a list of proposed values and distributed them to the employees, and asked people to vote for the ones they thought were most important. Carolan and his team analyzed the results, boiled the values down to a short list, and then went through another round of discussions with all 350 employees to refine the wording and make sure that the values they had selected were the ones that really mattered.

This broad and inclusive process proved to employees that their opinions and feelings mattered. As a result, they developed a much greater sense of ownership of the values than they would have with a list created by the leadership. As in most values-shaping efforts, the process itself was just as important as the specifics of the result, if not more so.

On our tour, Carolan pointed out one of the posters that hung throughout the facility. "Do what you say you are going to do," Carolan read aloud. "Maybe that sounds a little wordy, but it's what everybody wanted. We started with *Do what we say,* which felt fine to me, until someone asked: who is 'we'? It was a great question— people felt it might just be the leadership team! The dialogue we had about accountability and commitment helped us all understand each other better, and we ended up with perhaps a less elegant but more meaningful statement. *Do what you say you are going to do* applies to everybody. And it really helped drive performance."

With these values in place, Carolan shaped a straightforward strategy with just a few essential elements, each of which would require the team's execution capabilities. For each element, he identified one or two metrics. For example, in supply chain—a function often managed with many hard-to-decipher metrics—he had two: *service to our customers* and *pounds of soup per day* or, as they put it, *lbs/day.*

Service to our customers was a strategically important metric given the company's increased focus on large retailers with high expectations. Serving customers well was a source of pride, and the metric tapped into and reinforced that emotional energy to help drive coordination between shifts, efficiency improvements, and quality assurance.

Metrics That Motivate

The story behind lbs/day is even more intriguing. "At first," Carolan said, "we focused on *lbs/labor hour,* the standard way to measure how many pounds of soup the facility produced per hour worked. The problem was that the lbs/labor hour was meaningless to the team. It's hard to figure out what's a good number and what's bad and how people can individually make a difference in the number." Even worse, lbs/labor hour created some concern that management might try to improve that number by simply lowering the number of hours worked. "Of course, that wouldn't have made sense strategically because we were trying to grow volumes in our new plant. But many employees are paid by the hour and, as such, hours are critically important to them. That's how they pay the bills and put food on the table. Talk about a simple and absolutely essential learning!"

So Carolan and his team changed the metric to lbs/day. "Everyone handles the product—from preparation, to filling, to packaging and shipping," he said. "It's tangible and meaningful. And people can get excited when they see that number moving up. It also helps people coordinate and work together as one team. Pounds per day implies all shifts need to perform and help each other perform to maximize a day's production. Now the idea of cleaning and prepping for the next shift has taken on a whole new meaning. Everyone feels connected by lbs/day; they feel like part of the same effort to drive that metric." In other words, the lbs/day metric was meaningful at an individual level, and it also helped drive collaborative effort.

As successful as that metric proved to be, Carolan was careful not to add too many more of them. "You want a small number of metrics to create focus. When there is a proliferation of metrics in a bunch of detailed scorecards, it can be hard to ensure everyone is aligned on what really matters. The teams that win are the ones that figure out the short list that matter the most. Even so, you need enough metrics to make sure you're covering the range of what's important for the business and the people. Having a balanced set makes it more likely that everybody can find at least one that really motivates them." Essentially, Carolan was creating the right range of metrics to tap into different people's sources of pride while maintaining focus on what matters most.

Put Metrics in the Right Context

Another principle Carolan followed with the metrics was that communication about them had to be visible and clear. The five most important metrics were displayed on LCD screens throughout the facility in stoplight colors: green, yellow, and red—with the obvious implications that metrics in green are on target, yellow ones are in danger of getting off-track, and the red ones are below target. "If you have the right metrics, and suddenly one of them goes red, people instantly understand what it means and how they can help. That's often a frustration people have when they deal with overly analytical and abstract metrics—they don't know what they can do about it."

Carolan also uses ad hoc metrics and does so as thoughtfully as he employs the formal ones. "When we negotiate with big retailers, for example, cost becomes very important. I tried a *pennies/lb* metric with the employees, but it was hard for them to care about a penny when they accidentally spilled some soup or dropped an ingredient. So instead, I used *pennies/lb* to talk about how our performance on that metric had made a difference in winning or losing a customer's business. When people understood that we could win or lose a big sale because of a few pennies, they paid a lot more attention." Carolan not only tapped into the team's pride in winning customers and growing volume, he also tapped into their informal connections—no one wanted to let down the sales team that was out there working hard to land a big contract.

Being Nice Doesn't Drive Performance

Ed Carolan believes that creating personal connections to the work helps build and maintain a high level of performance, but makes it clear that it is *measurable* performance results that matter most. The energy and enthusiasm that we witnessed on our plant tour are great but are ultimately meaningless if they do not move the performance needle in a positive direction.

"Ed's approach reminds me of high school," one of his direct reports told us. "I had a chemistry teacher who treated all his students like kindergartners. She would put a smiley face on your paper if she thought it was good. I really hated her. I didn't do the work. I didn't engage with her. My calculus teacher, however, treated us like adults. He expected us to do 'A' work and you didn't want to disappoint him. I got much better grades in his class than in chemistry. Ed is like that calculus teacher. He engages the team and gets us to engage with each other. But he expects us to work really hard and deliver our personal best! That has built trust and we don't want to disappoint him."

At the end of our day at the StockPot facility, we walked with Carolan to the parking lot. As he climbed onto his motorcycle, a worker came out of the plant.

"Hey, Ed!" the worker called out.

"Hey!" Carolan called back.

"I hear we made more soup last Saturday than we ever have! Is that true?"

"That's right," Carolan shouted. "Highest daily production in StockPot history."

"Yes!" the worker called out, did a quick fist pump, and let out a whoop.

Carolan smiled, we said goodnight, and he roared away. Clearly, the efforts he had put into galvanizing his team around performance were paying off.

MOTIVATING FROM THE SIDE

Ed Carolan's success at StockPot was the result of his unrelenting insistence on performance—both individual and group—and his ability to employ metrics in different ways that were meaningful to his employees. But what if Carolan needed to turn around performance without the formal authority he had as an executive? Would that approach work?

In today's flattening world, it is increasingly common that leaders need to drive performance without formal authority. This is particularly true in outsourcing situations, joint ventures, and loose business affiliations (like airline alliances)—anywhere that managers are responsible for departments or functions outside their official lines and boxes. Consider the following intriguing quote from the *New York Times*:

> The people who truly succeed in business are the ones who actually have figured out how to mobilize people who are not their direct reports. Everyone can get their direct reports to work for them, but getting people who do not have to give you their time to engage and to support you and to want you to succeed is something that is sorely missing from B-school courses.[1]

But how can people motivate behavior change and performance in groups that they don't formally manage? This is exactly the kind of situation in which the informal organization is absolutely essential.

Informal Carrots Deliver What Formal Sticks Cannot

In the autumn of 2004, Gregg Sheehy, a contract relationship executive and senior vice president at Bank of America (BofA), took over responsibility for the bank's relationship with TeleTech, an independent customer support call center to which BofA outsourced much of its helpline business.

In fact, TeleTech's thousand customer service reps fielded some 60 percent of the calls made to BofA's customer support line. As Sheehy put it, "For all intents and purposes, the voice of TeleTech was the voice of BofA." But, although TeleTech handled the largest volume of calls of any of the bank's ten customer service centers, it also had the lowest performance record in terms of customer delight.

Sheehy needed to improve TeleTech's performance, but he had no formal authority over the company. TeleTech's people didn't work for Sheehy; he was not their manager. The contract between BofA and TeleTech only covered the minimum expectations that TeleTech needed to meet. Sheehy might have been able to cancel the contract, but that would have caused huge disruption to service and probably involved endless legal hassles as well.

So, Sheehy had very few, if any, formal sticks available to him. He decided that he would have to work with informal carrots instead. He'd have to find ways to motivate TeleTech's employees and persuade them to exceed the minimum expectations laid out in the contract. To that end, he would first have to figure out what the TeleTech workforce needed from BofA. And to do that, he would have to make a visit to the center to see for himself how it operated.

Making the Right Connections

"The second I walked in the door of the call center," Sheehy told us, "I could tell there was a credibility issue. I learned that three other BofA execs had been responsible for the center in the past year alone." According to the TeleTech people Sheehy talked with, the BofA executives had made their inspections, talked earnestly about the relationship and how important it was, and then left, never to be heard from again. "So when I asked the TeleTech people what I could do to gain credibility, they all said the same thing, 'Stay in the job!'"

Sheehy set out to build a different type of relationship than his predecessors had. For starters, he gave the TeleTech employees his word that he wasn't going anywhere. During the first few months, Sheehy visited TeleTech every other week. He wanted the people to know that he was interested both in results and in the people who worked at the company. "I needed them to know that I was watching, and that I cared," Sheehy says.

On his visits, Sheehy would walk the floor and talk with customer service reps. He built relationships with members of the leadership team and other key influencers. He took them out for meals, shared stories, paid attention to what mattered to them, and, as a result, got to know them personally. Pretty soon he was almost as much a part of their world as if he actually worked in their company.

In an arm's-length relationship like the one between client and supplier, the client is always very tempted to be as efficient as possible. After all, it's the client's time that's valuable—not the other way around. Instead, Sheehy took the route of short-term inefficiency to gain long-term improvement in performance. His investment up front with face time gave him plenty of relationship capital that he could draw on later, as needed.

Meaningful Aspirations Motivate

As mutual respect increased, Gregg Sheehy was able to get the employees to see more clearly the need to close the performance gap. He convinced them that rather than accept the minimal level of service laid out in their contract, they should aspire to exceed the contractual agreements and take personal pride in the achievement.

With TeleTech's leadership, Sheehy set a goal of becoming the number one call center at BofA based on customer delight—a lofty goal for a call center that had consistently been the lowest performer. However, Sheehy wanted TeleTech employees to believe they could move beyond their current performance level.

"I knew this wasn't going to be easy for them," Sheehy told us. "In order to be number one they'd have to cut costs—partially through a reduction in headcount—and improve their performance on several metrics that had been at low levels for some time."

If Sheehy had walked in TeleTech's door on his first visit and announced that the company had to become number one by such-and-such a date, it's doubtful that he would have gotten much traction. However, because the employees had come to know and trust him, and believed in his commitment to them, they began to like the idea of "going for the top spot."

Nobody really wants to be second best.

Personal, Credible Interactions Are Mandatory

Gregg Sheehy believed the key to demonstrating both his and BofA's commitment to TeleTech's ability to improve was continued personal support and close, informal contact. No matter where he was, or what time zone he was in, Sheehy called in to offer his personal congratulations whenever a new benchmark had been achieved. He also asked that the entire call center, not just the leadership team, get together to participate in these calls.

This practice occasionally took a personal toll on Sheehy, who was a frequent global traveler. Once, while on a business trip to China, he was notified about an exceptional performance accomplishment at TeleTech. He wanted to congratulate everybody, which meant scheduling a call during a shift change. The only time he could arrange that was at 3 AM local China time. The fact that Sheehy would make a call at that hour made his words of congratulation all the more meaningful to the TeleTech employees. In just a few months, TeleTech's call center rose from last place to first place among BofA's call centers.

This is a striking example of how a manager who has very little formal authority can quickly improve performance by leading outside the lines—in this case the lines that distinguish client and supplier. In our lexicon, Gregg Sheehy's approach was to balance the formal imperatives with informal mechanisms in ways that would create the emotional commitment and energy needed to change behaviors to push TeleTech up the ladder of performance results.

As companies turn to outsourcing as a solution for a greater number of strategic and financial challenges, the limits of formal contractual interactions become more and more apparent. But the emotional interactions of the informal organization and its power to motivate performance are ever-present and available, even across institutional lines.

Like Ken Mehlman in Chapter Four, Ed Carolan at StockPot and Gregg Sheehy at Bank of America were able to motivate their people to higher levels of performance, not by enslaving workers with rigid top-down metrics *or* by being nice to all and making friends. Their approaches were neither hard nor soft. Instead they took the best of both the formal and informal organizations and integrated them to drive their people and partners to a shared purpose.

CLEAR OBJECTIVES HELP EVERYONE CONTRIBUTE

Kyle Ewalt worked at Katzenbach Partners in the firm's New York City office as service center manager. He is a vivid exemplar for those who are relentlessly focused on the objective of realizing the sometimes impossible requests that arise when serving clients. Though Ewalt worked full time, he also performed and composed music outside work. He is over six and a half feet tall, slender, and always has a smile on his face, not to mention an attractive beard that everyone likes to tease him about. After Ewalt had been with Katzenbach Partners for nearly five years, he was formally recognized by the entire firm with a Values Award, which was given to the person who was considered to be the most effective in delivering client impact.

This was surprising, since Ewalt was not a consultant and did not serve clients directly. Yet he was judged by his colleagues to have a more positive, consistent impact on the firm's clients than anyone else (including consultants, partners, and managers), across the firm's four main geographic locations. His influence far exceeded any formal responsibility or authority.

A prime example of Ewalt's impact was provided in the winter of 2006, when the firm hosted a photo shoot at our office for a client. We had never done anything like it before and it turned out to be a more complicated task than any of us had expected. For example, during the preparations for the shoot there were some miscommunications with the photographer. As a result, when the photographer arrived on the morning of the shoot, it was discovered that a crucial piece of equipment was missing: a roll of backdrop paper.

There was still an hour to go before the clients arrived, so— rather than cancel the shoot, subject the clients to a lot of stress, and incur the expense of rescheduling—Ewalt immediately set to work. Through his informal connections, he located a backdrop of the precise specifications required at a photo supply company across town. Rather than rely on a delivery service, he jumped in a cab and went to pick up the backdrop himself. Unfortunately, the scroll was fourteen feet long and wouldn't fit in a cab. No problem for Ewalt; he perched it on his shoulder and carried it back to the office on foot. The backdrop was in place when the clients arrived. The shoot went off without a hitch. The clients were thrilled, and they never knew the lengths that Ewalt had gone to. In fact, they never even learned his name.

Kyle Ewalt's informal capability was recognized as an important one to the firm and that it should be scaled up. We established a Service Center, led by Ewalt and staffed by a small team of people who performed functions similar to the ones he had previously done by himself. Ewalt is a remarkable example of a person that no one in our firm wanted to disappoint—and it had nothing whatsoever to do with his formal authority.

THE INFORMAL BUILDS PERFORMANCE; PERFORMANCE ENHANCES THE INFORMAL

Both the formal and informal organizations are needed to reach performance goals and both are strengthened by doing so. Managers can encourage this kind of mutual reinforcement in a number of ways:

1. *Set group performance goals* that require people to collaborate and often experience life in a real team. By working together, they get to know each other's values, skills, aspirations, and feelings. Even after the collaborative groups disband, the relationships remain as an asset to be tapped into down the road. Having common as well as individual goals also allows you to motivate team as well as individual performance.

2. *Make goals meaningful* to motivate create a sense of purpose and striving. When a goal is made individually meaningful, it becomes a source of pride. People develop pride in the journey, and success leads to pride in accomplishments. Meaningful performance goals will always be challenging, and that allows the group members to further build pride as they achieve them.

3. *Apply values to the hardest problems* that stand in the way of achieving performance goals. Simple analytical techniques often won't suffice for the hard problems—otherwise they would be easy problems. When applying values enables progress and the resolution of important problems, it reinforces the usefulness of those values as a group experience. This further embeds them and makes them more

useful to solving the next problem and improving performance. The confidence that comes from solving these hardest problems allows groups to become more aspirational in setting the next set of performance goals.

· · · · · · · · ·

Of course, this is all about improving performance results. Yet we don't seem to act like we know that when it comes to the informal organization. We can track the performance results of the formal organization because changes in strategies, structures, and processes are readily measurable. When it comes to the informal, however, we fall back on opinion surveys and fuzzy measures of engagement. While we might assume that good scores in people's attitudes will lead to performance results, we cannot say for sure.

That's not good enough anymore. At first, changes in the informal elements seem hard to link directly to improvements in sales, margins, costs, and market share. In reality they are not—you can link those changes directly to specific behaviors. Moreover, informally boosted behavior changes can be linked directly to performance results, if in no other way by rigorous pilot tests. In the Bell Canada situation described in Chapter Eight, for example, Michael Sabia's team ran several pilot tests that confirmed sales and margin gains stemming directly from the behaviors that were motivated by the informal pride movement. In Shell's refinery system, similar pilot tests confirmed that informally motivated behaviors led to measurable changes in downtimes and maintenance recovery rates. And the remarkable Aetna turnaround described in Chapter Nine was led by the integration of informal and formal leadership behaviors, and was in marked contrast to the formally driven shortfalls that preceded the effort.

So don't take our word for it, prove it to yourself if you are still in doubt. Activate informal mechanisms aimed at a few behaviors you know should improve your results and put it to the test one way or another. Performance results are what this is all about, so make sure you get them.

PART THREE

MOBILIZING ORGANIZATIONAL CHANGE

Certain individuals have higher organizational quotients than others—that is, they instinctively (or through years of trial and error) know how to tap into both informal and formal elements to accelerate behavior change and performance results—and are often willing to break a few rules to do so.

A wise leader will learn from these high-OQ people, modify inflexible rules to alleviate barriers, and help others balance the formal with the informal. By amplifying what's already working, and by applying a few proven principles for integrating the formal with the informal organization, leaders can accelerate significant transformations in performance results. And when they blend the informal with the formal changes, they produce results that last longer than traditional change management programs that leave the informal to instinct and chance.

In Part Three, we introduce the notion of "fast zebras" and how to capitalize on their seemingly magical sense of how to blend the informal with the formal. We have found them in all kinds of organizational settings, even in the most formal. They bring their wisdom to small businesses, large corporate bureaucracies, political campaigns, and public school systems. Now we take you a bit further into some of these diverse organizational challenges.

Chapter Ten, which ends the book, is about what to do—a discussion of specific actions and practices to employ in getting the best from both the formal and informal organizations.

● ● ● ● ● ● ● ● ●

7

Setting the Fast Zebras Free

I t is hard for those who have not personally experienced the working environment of the United Nations to fully appreciate the
bureaucratic protocols, matrixed structures, process complexity, and
multicultural influences at play there. However, it is not hard to
imagine how difficult it must be to get anything done efficiently in an
organization as complicated as the UN. Nor is it difficult to picture
the frustrations that a newcomer must feel in trying to understand
which players need to be involved, when, and for what purpose,
just to get something done. Add to this the fact that most political
appointees are in their positions for a short period of time, and you
can begin to see why figuring out how to navigate the informal waters
is essential.

We were fortunate enough to meet with Mark D. Wallace, U.S.
Ambassador to the United Nations during the Bush administration,
who painted for us an informal portrait of how the UN works. Wallace
understands very well the challenges involved and explained to us
how he worked to balance the many competing interests that existed
within his office and across the entire organization of the UN.

Wallace was well prepared for his UN experience. He began
his work in government as a private lawyer working for the City of

Miami Emergency Financial Oversight Board. After taking part in the 2000 presidential election recount and the Homeland Security departmental reconfiguration, he joined the 2004 presidential reelection campaign as deputy campaign manager, with responsibilities that included, among other things, acting as message manager for the Republican convention. Following the GOP's unexpected victory, President George W. Bush appointed him to the U.S. mission to the United Nations. With charismatic good humor, Wallace talked with us about his role as a political appointee, and the challenges that accompany it. "One of the advantages of winning," he joked, "is that, Democrat or Republican, there are a number of positions that will always be filled by the people—hopefully the best people—who got you there."

However, the world one enters as an appointee to the UN is very different from life on the campaign trail, where the speed and unpredictability of events create an often haphazard and highly informal environment. This places a premium on rapid responsiveness, high tolerance for uncertainty, and perhaps a love of ambiguity. There is always a tremendous amount of work to be done, and so, as Wallace says, "It becomes very clear, very quickly, who the fast zebras are."

Fast zebras is one of Wallace's favorite metaphors for those people who have the ability to absorb information and adapt to sudden challenges capably and quickly. On the African savannah, it is the fast zebra that survives a visit to the watering hole, drinking quickly and moving on, while the slower herd members fall prey to predators lurking in the shadows.

The fast zebra is, in essence, a person who knows how to draw on both the formal and informal organizations with equal facility. As a manager, Wallace knew that recruiting those people who helped him in the extremely informal environment of the presidential campaign would very likely be able to help him in the extremely formal bureaucracy he would have to negotiate as a political appointee to the UN.

To give us a better understanding of the nature of the fast zebra, Wallace introduced us to one of his most treasured associates, Henley MacIntyre. She began as a volunteer intern on the campaign, quickly rose through the organization, and worked closely with Wallace at the convention. After the election and a stint at the White House, she joined him at the UN.

MacIntyre has an outgoing personality and Texas-style charm that are immediately disarming. And, as she explains, all her charm was necessary at the UN as well as on the campaign trail. When MacIntyre joined the 2004 campaign, it was her first job out of college, and her first job in Washington. "I was really green," she readily admits. But her desk was right outside Wallace's office and she immediately saw that he "always treated his team as equals and was sure to give credit and positive reinforcement whenever possible." This made MacIntyre eager to please the boss, and she felt no qualms about putting in sixty-hour weeks.

Wallace was, indeed, extremely pleased with MacIntyre's performance and soon promoted her to be his assistant. Then, as the convention approached, MacIntyre spotted a crisis in the making. With only four days to go before delegates began to arrive, Henley and a colleague learned that the movements—arrivals, departures, appearances, seating arrangements—for many of the speakers and other "big dogs" who would be attending the convention had yet to be adequately coordinated. This work was not part of MacIntyre's formal job description (she didn't really have one, anyway) and she wasn't sure if it might be someone else's responsibility. No matter. MacIntyre took on the task herself. She spent the next four days on the phone, figuring out who should arrive when, where they should sit, and who couldn't sit next to each other for political reasons. It involved navigating a complicated web of networks. Not only did MacIntyre manage to understand and organize it, she made herself a part of it, personally connecting with many big donors and other players throughout the convention.

MacIntyre's ability, commitment, and good humor impressed not only Wallace but also the White House political director, and her savvy and execution in the clutch of the convention won her an offer for a position in the White House. While Wallace knew it would be to her advantage to take on such a high-profile role, he told her that anytime she wanted to join his staff when he moved to the UN, she had a place. Sure enough, after she had spent several months in Washington, and a few months after Wallace took up his position at the UN, MacIntyre decided to bring her talents to New York and the international arena of the United Nations.

Bringing Agility to the UN

MacIntyre's rise is a classic example of what a fast zebra can accomplish in a fast-paced and high-intensity environment. It is also a great example of how important one's informal sensitivity can be when the situation is complicated by an entrenched bureaucratic culture. Transferring the informal talents that helped during the campaign to an appointee's position in the highly formalized world of international diplomacy was a challenge that required Wallace and MacIntyre to stretch their informal organization muscles. MacIntyre astutely saw where the lines were, and she led outside them when necessary.

As Wallace explains, two types of people work at the UN, and they are fundamentally different: political appointees and their staff, who are there for relatively limited periods of time, and the Foreign Service career staff members, who may spend their entire professional lives working at the UN. An appointee has comparatively little time to effect lasting positive change. For example, most major change efforts in the business world require several years to accomplish; most political appointees are in the job for fewer than two years. As a result, Wallace found it was crucial to have access to his own herd of fast zebras who could build credibility as well as act and adapt quickly. There is no time for training or gradual acclimation to the role—selection of the right people, like MacIntyre, is crucial.

With the aid of a core team of fast zebras, Wallace was able to institute significant change, beginning in his own shop. He started by trying to remove some formal obstacles, such as the use of cumbersome briefing booklets as background for dialogues and major decisions. The creation of these books, sometimes hundreds of pages long, had become institutionalized over the years as the best way to catalogue and convey useful information throughout the formal hierarchy. Obviously, their original purpose was long gone.

Wallace knew that before he could do away with—or even significantly modify—this antiquated process, he and his team would have to gain the respect of their colleagues who had long relied on these briefing books and still believed in their value. To do so, Wallace decided he would have to prove two things: first, that his team could produce good briefing books in the traditional manner; and second, that they could develop a better, faster way to internalize and master the same massive quantities of information, without the "bugsmasher" book.

While clearly not as simple as it sounds, the new system worked and saved the U.S. mission countless hours. It also freed up Wallace's staff to research new topics instead of covering well-worn ground. He worked hard to show his people that he'd rather have them suggest and carry out their own research than prep him, and this empowered and energized long-term staffers and appointees alike. At the same time, Wallace attributes much of this success to the respect he and his team showed to those who had favored the old system. They acted collectively as fast zebras to achieve a result that Wallace would have found hard to achieve otherwise.

Informal behaviors that demonstrate respect, humility, and humor, Wallace says, are key tools for his fast zebras, as well as for his own interactions at the UN. These are probably at least as important as formal skills that reflect a person's intelligence, experience, and education. Given his operating style on the campaign trail or in his shop, Wallace isn't afraid to jump into the trenches and get his hands dirty. He doesn't routinely submit to the traditional hierarchies of the diplomatic service. He believes that far more mileage can be gained by treating everyone equally and respectfully.

Wallace's informal savvy paid off in very tangible ways. For example, during the course of events at the UN, it sometimes happens that a country delegation—one that had been encouraged to vote against a U.S. sponsored initiative—breaks ranks and becomes a U.S. ally on a vote, simply due to the respect Wallace showed its ambassador in the hallway. By the same token, the United States must play its role deftly. As a superpower, the United States is often the target of animosity and resentment. But to remain effective and avoid antagonizing those who are predetermined obstructionists, U.S. ambassadors need to maintain deference and propriety, even in the face of belligerence. When you are, as Wallace describes it, "the hegemon," you have to remain above the fray, or risk exacerbating an already delicate situation. And just as humor can be an asset in the high-stress environment of a political campaign, it can also be an advantageous weapon in one's debate arsenal.

While Wallace recognizes that the U.S. position often makes it difficult for his team to get things done, he also makes good use of the difficulty, and turns that challenge into a source of pride. For example, before large meetings, he and his staff will sometimes do their fun version of a Maori haka (a war dance of New Zealand origin). Wallace knows that his fast zebras thrive on overcoming obstacles—as they did in the realm of the political campaign—so he tries to rally, motivate, and energize them in their new, intensely hierarchical environment by creating the same sense of tackling an impossible mission. Prior to a recent vote, Wallace says, he exclaimed, "A hundred ninety-one nations against one. I like our odds!"

As an appointee, Wallace spent only a short amount of time at the UN, but his informal instincts will undoubtedly have a lasting impact on the U.S. mission and the entire organization, as he left behind a crisp example for others to follow. Informal and fast zebra techniques were ultimately effective at cracking the code of success at the UN, despite its legacy of tradition and hierarchy.

• • • • • • • • •

Clearly, fast zebras can help the stiff joints of overly formal organizations move smoothly again. They help the formal organization get unstuck when surprises come its way, or when it's time to head in a new direction. They have the ability to understand how the organization works, and the street smarts to figure out how to get around stubborn obstacles. They draw on values and personal relationships to help people make choices that align with overall strategy and get around misguided policy. They draw on networks to form teams that collaborate on problems not owned by any formal structure. They tap into different sources of pride to motivate the behaviors ignored by formal reward systems.

However, it can be lonely to be the only fast zebra at the watering hole. So wise leaders identify their fast zebras and help create conditions that will attract more of their kind. By creating a herd, leaders can accelerate more quickly and on a broader scale than any one fast zebra could on its own.

MOBILIZING THE RIGHT CROWDS TO TRANSFORM PS 130

In 1990, when Lily Din Woo was brought in to replace the outgoing principal of the Hernando DeSoto School, PS 130 in Manhattan's Chinatown, the school was barely meeting the state-mandated performance requirements. It was on the brink of becoming a SURR school (School under Registration Review), meaning that it would be placed on the academic failure list. Continuation on this list would lead to restructuring or even closure. To make matters worse, Woo was a surprise choice for the position. The school community had assumed that the long-serving and well-liked assistant principal would get the job. Who was this Lily Woo, coming in from the outside?

Today, PS 130 is considered one of the best public elementary schools in New York, regularly scoring in the top 10 percent. Woo is recognized as one of the most successful and innovative principals in the public school system. And the school community respects and even loves her. It was a remarkable turnaround, indeed.

How did Woo accomplish it? By tapping into informal school networks and changing the balance in what had been an overly formal organization. There is no doubt that Woo has a very high OQ—she has a formidable mastery of the formal school structures and processes, as well as a deep understanding of the strong social networks that exist within a public institution of education. In her earlier life, she was almost certainly a fast zebra—and she has not forgotten those insights.

The Crowd Was Against Her to Start

The Department of Education in New York City is a complex bureaucracy that has long frustrated principals and other educators who have wanted to make reforms or institute innovations. The system demands that teachers and administrators follow the rules, adhere to procedures, and complete mountains of paperwork—even if the formalities seem to get in the way of the system's primary mission: to ensure that every member of an incredibly diverse student body receives a good education. What's more, the system is sharply divided into constituencies that don't always see eye to eye. Parents,

the teachers' union, school administration, system administration—
and, oh yes, students—often found themselves at odds with each
other, working at cross-purposes, and even in direct confrontation.

Woo knew all this, of course, when she took over as principal.
She also knew that, to avoid the possibility of closure, PS 130 could
not continue to operate as it had been. Something had to give.

What she did not expect, however, was the frigid reception she
would get when she came aboard. She had worked for decades in the
public school system—as a teacher, staff developer, and administrator—and she was a well-known member of the Chinatown community. None of that mattered. Woo was an outsider to PS 130 and
had elbowed aside the beloved assistant principal. Many parents and
teachers felt so negatively about Woo's appointment that they made
formal protest to the school authorities.

Clearly, Woo had to win over the faculty, the administration,
the teachers' union, and the parents, which was going to be an uphill
battle. She accomplished it, over a period of years, by making formal changes and by drawing on informal networks. For example,
Woo cut costs, one of the most traditional formal mechanisms of
change. She made sure, however, to include her own office in the
cost-cutting, by reducing the number of secretaries in the principal's
office from three to one.

She articulated her own informal set of educational standards—to supplement the formal metrics of the public system—and
distributed them to and discussed them at length with all teachers.
The standards had to do with innovation, information sharing, and
connecting with students.

Woo identified the school's main areas of weakness in the educational program and worked tirelessly to improve them. For example, she found that many of the students at PS 130 struggled with
the English language and that the language skills curriculum was
not up to snuff, so she fought for resources to improve the teaching

of English. To build better relationships with parents, she offered free English classes for adults, which she taught herself until a few sympathetic teachers volunteered to help her.

PS 130 parents had long complained that the math curriculum was too easy for their children, so Woo found ways to make it better meet the students' needs and align better with the parents' expectations. To improve her standing with teachers, she helped to design a much more flexible and comprehensive skills development program. Gradually, the tide turned.

As Woo gained the trust of the different constituencies and created links among them, she found that amazing things could happen. As test scores rose and programs were added and expanded, the Parents Association voluntarily hosted a Chinese banquet. Not only did the event publicly celebrate the school's success, the admission fees were used to create a fund to support further improvement to the curriculum. (The banquet is now held annually and raises some $90,000 per year for the school.)

With the proceeds from other intensified fundraising efforts, Woo was able to start up new enrichment programs for students, including arts classes (traditionally underfunded by the city). Moreover, the school community grew into a much more cohesive social network. It became a wise and collaborative crowd, rather than an angry, divisive one.

"The credit lies with Principal Lily Woo," as one third-grade parent said. "She manages to combine a genius for fiscal management with the hands-on involvement that finds her sitting at the door of the school every morning greeting her 1000+ students by name."[1]

Gradually and with great determination, Woo managed to create a virtuous cycle. Every time she drew on her informal network to navigate the formal labyrinth, the success of her efforts strengthened the network still further. Part of this success had to do with Woo's ability to know when to try new ways of doing things. "It's like

GPS—if you're on the wrong route, you have to find a way back to a road that will lead you to the location you want to get to. If you force yourself to go down only one road, you're going to hit a ditch or a dead end, and then what?"

The Storeroom Bottleneck

The story of the storeroom at PS 130 provides a good example of Woo's ability to find a new route around a very old and divisive problem. She found it thanks to a basic problem and the resulting revelation—both as obvious and fundamental as Ed Carolan's realization about the importance of hours to the StockPot employees.

It all started when Woo's chair broke. "One of the wheels fell off and I couldn't get it back on, so I bought myself a new chair. The faculty said, how could you buy yourself a fancy new chair? We need this, and we need that. And it dawned on me. Duh. They need stuff."

But to get the supplies they needed, teachers had to go through an elaborate and antiquated formal process. "There was a supply lady, and there were supplies," Woo said. "But I didn't understand the system of how the supplies were given out. The teacher would say to the supply person, 'I need chalk.' And she would give out two pieces of chalk. Or, 'I need paper.' And the supply lady would ask, 'How many children do you have in your class? Thirty? Here's thirty sheets of paper.' If you used up your thirty sheets and went back for more, it was, 'Sorry, you've used up September's allotment.'"

So Woo went down to the storage room to take a look for herself. "I saw a whole room full of stuff. Paper that was turning yellow. There was a hoarding going on, a saving. The supply people were afraid that we were never going to have stuff again. So I took apart the supply closet and just gave out everything. I said, 'You need paper?' Here's two reams. 'You need chalk?' Take the whole box."

The supply officer was horrified. "She said, 'You can't do that! You can't do that!' But I said, 'Who said? This stuff is meant to be used. We can buy new stuff.'" Next, Woo examined the budget and found that there were too many people involved in the purchasing process. "It was one of those things where you're keeping two or three people to keep the last one who's doing the work of the four people. So I really kept on top of the people who needed to do work, and they didn't like it, and they left."

Instead of replacing those people, Woo transferred the budget to purchasing, but did the allocation of funds very differently from before. "For instance, we would get an allocation of $50,000 to spend on books. We have fifty teachers. Fifty teachers divided into fifty thousand—everybody gets $1,000. Seems equal and fair, but it's really not. If you've been teaching twenty-six years, you've accumulated stuff. If you're a brand new teacher, you're going to need more support. So I started a wish list with them. They said, 'What do you mean a wish list?' I said, 'A wish list. Tell me what you need.'"

In prior days, if the teachers knew about a $50,000 allocation and their $1,000 piece of it, they would find a way to spend the money, even if they didn't need anything. "No teacher is going to be so generous as to say, 'You know what, Lily, I don't need my $1,000. You can give it to him.' Instead, you look through every catalog. 'Let me see how I can spend $1,000 exactly.' Or maybe there is something you really need that costs $1,050. You've only got $1,000, so you can't buy it. So you buy other stuff just to spend your $1,000. So, we started with a wish list. And they said, 'Well, how much are you giving us?' I said, 'I'm not telling you how much. Tell me what you want. And we'll talk about it.' And so we slowly started shifting, putting the money where it was needed."

Why don't more people look for alternate routes around obvious formal bottlenecks? "They don't know any better," Woo says. "They're afraid to think outside the box, to ask, 'Can I do this?' And if there's nothing that says you can't, then you can."

Making Magic Beyond PS 130

Today, thanks to Woo's efforts and those of her administration and faculty, PS 130 has become a model for other schools in the city system.

The school chancellors, whose formalities Woo often battled against early on, have embraced her and her methods. And, frustrated by their own excessive red tape and administrative roadblocks, they have begun several initiatives to mobilize informal social networks.

Eric Nadelstern, the Head of the Empowerment Program for the New York City Department of Education, told us that he thinks of Woo's approach as "creative noncompliance." In a system that had long been authoritarian and hierarchical, Nadelstern and his colleagues came to believe, thanks largely to Woo's example, that "autonomy is not a reward for having achieved success; it is a requirement of achieving success."

This is a radical change of attitude for the Department of Education. Formerly, each school belonged to a geographic district, led by a superintendent. All the principals in the district reported directly to the superintendent whose rules and regulations they were expected to follow.

This system had, Nadelstern says, "no accountability for results, only compliance with the rules." The principal who wanted career advancement knew that the best way to do so was to adhere to the rules and satisfy the superintendent; the school's educational performance was almost irrelevant.

The formal rules had their advantages, of course. They brought consistency and homogeneity to a system that previously had been a somewhat haphazard collection of schools with differing approaches and varying degrees of quality. Throughout the American public educational system, homogeneity has long been considered to be a good thing. The theory was that if every school had access to the same influences, every child would turn out the same.

But, as principals like Lily Woo—those with high OQ—proved that their creative noncompliance and individuated solutions almost always brought better results, Eric Nadelstern and his colleagues realized that a change in certain aspects of the formal organization—rather than a simple enhancement of the informal—was required. "Because people are all different, schools need to accommodate those differences," Nadelstern told us. "It's basic human nature. We had gone to an ingenious level to perfect a scalable but flawed educational model. The district-based system could not simply be incrementally reformed to match this shift in thinking, it had to be almost literally blown up and started again."

The Empowerment Program

In 2006, New York initiated a program designed to give more independence to principals who had proved themselves to be masters of the informal organization. Called the Empowerment program, it was meant to give decision-making authority to those who worked more directly with students. Principals, for example, were given greater flexibility for making decisions about curriculum and more freedom to allocate their financial resources as they saw fit. Most received a $100,000 discretionary fund.

In exchange for their new freedoms, the principals were to be held to a higher degree of accountability for the overall success of their schools and were required to sign agreements that included performance targets for a four-year period. In its first year, Empowerment schools performed better on average than the rest of New York's public schools, scoring significantly higher on standardized math and reading exams. At the time of our interviews, 332 principals had agreed to participate in the Empowerment initiative.

To many educators, Empowerment represents a revolution rather than a mere reform. Principals no longer report to superintendents. Rather the DOE's Empowerment support team reports to the principals—around twenty of them—who constitute a network, rather than a geographic district. The network support team works for the principals, helping them with curriculum changes, staff development, and budgeting. The formal expression of the change is that the administrator's bonuses are determined, not by the chancellors or the higher administration, but by the principals they serve.

The composition of the network has nothing to do with geography or grade level. Most networks are composed of schools located in a number of different boroughs and span Kindergarten through Grade 12. Principals often join a particular network because they want to work with its support team. Others join a network because it contains like-minded principals.

The Empowerment program not only granted more autonomy to principals, it enabled them to enhance their networks by giving them opportunities to connect with principals from all over the city. It also created a pride audience, in that the principals develop respect for others in their network and are loath to disappoint them. Simply put, members of the networks instilled pride in one another's efforts and achievements.

One final note: it's important to reiterate that Lily Woo did not *reject* the formal organization. She retained what worked best about the formal and found ways to fill the gaps and shortfalls with informal solutions. The proof that Woo's high-OQ methods are working lies not only in her school's performance but also in the support she has built among teachers, parents, and the Department of Education.

Woo's teachers became so dedicated to her that they were sometimes willing to teach as unpaid volunteers. One teacher asked to come on board three months before Woo expected to have the funding to pay him, just to be a part of her school.

Parents demonstrated their dedication to Woo by nominating her as an "everyday hero" with the Summer Olympics Committee in 2004. The letter they wrote earned her a spot as one of New York's Olympic torch carriers that year.

And the DOE believed in Lily Woo so strongly that it invited PS 130 to be one of the pilot schools of the Empowerment network. She is a big fan of the program. "My staff loves it because they feel that we're not beholden to anyone but ourselves. It really allows us to do what we need to do, without somebody hovering over us and saying, 'you must do this initiative.' We choose our initiatives, and we choose how we go about doing it."

· · · · · · · · ·

Fast zebras can be found in all kinds of organizations, and in many different roles. They are, however, still relatively rare animals. Obviously, a wise leader learns to recognize and use them effectively. They have the ability to navigate treacherous waters of complex organizations, as well as the wisdom to cultivate the informal relationships that will guide them to perform well. What is more important, however, is that even though the instinctive fast zebras are rare, most people in most organizations have the potential to improve those skills.

It boils down to paying closer attention to the informal elements in your organization. We all network informally to some extent. We don't all, however, think rigorously about who we might add to our networks to enrich our work experience, or how we might more effectively influence those within our networks to help us perform better.

A few fast zebras, like Henley MacIntyre, are born that way or master their skills early on. Others, like Lily Woo, master them the

hard way, through years of trial and error under difficult circumstances. We believe, however, that most people can improve their
organizational effectiveness and performance significantly by learning how to connect emotionally as well as rationally with a few more
of their respected colleagues.

8

Melting the Frozen Tundra

Does the following sequence sound familiar?

- Set an objective.
- Develop an action plan to achieve objective.
- Push forward execution of plan.
- Realize that plan is not working.
- Push harder with action plan.
- Find that objective is not being met.
- Push even harder with action plan.
- Watch as people abandon ship.
- Redefine objective and declare victory.

If this sounds familiar, it's not surprising. Far too often, this is how companies approach the implementation of strategy, change programs, and all sorts of other business initiatives—and why so many of them fail. Their leaders refuse to accept a basic truth that Scottish bard Robbie Burns famously described, "The best laid schemes o' mice an' men / gang aft agley."

Or, in other words, stuff happens.

The formal organization doesn't like change. And that's mostly a good thing—the predictability and repeatability of the formal organization are among its key benefits. Once the formal is set up and humming along, people become comfortable with their goals, formal power, and repeatable processes. So it's natural for the formal to freeze up when things run amok—as they inevitably do.

So how can organizations get out of the loop of "push harder"? How can companies change their approach to "set goals, develop plans, execute, whoa! that was interesting, adapt plan, execute differently . . ."

That's where the informal organization comes in. Let's look at what one leader accomplished at Bell Canada.

SEEDING A MOVEMENT

In 2003, we met with Michael Sabia, the CEO of Bell Canada. A mutual colleague arranged the meeting, and told us that Sabia was hoping to discuss the challenge he had with his top team. However, when we broached that topic, Sabia shook his head. "My problem isn't at the top. It's across the bottom," he told us.

"The bottom?" Not what we had expected.

"The organization's stuck. We introduced all sorts of well-planned strategic, organization, and operating programs, but very few have had the impact we need. The front line is not changing their actions and behavior nearly as fast as we need, so we know we're doing something wrong." Then he added, "To make matters worse, many of my leaders are not convinced that we need to change our approach. They want to keep pushing the programs. Sometimes it seems like trying to pound through frozen tundra."

His choice of words was revealing: *frozen tundra*.

Sabia was an insightful strategist with a long, successful career working in government. He'd engineered a massive turnaround at Canadian National Railroad, making him the perfect candidate to help the ailing Bell Canada. When he became CEO in 2002, he walked into a mess. His predecessor had jumped on the multimedia bandwagon and launched new businesses much too rapidly. This left the company overextended, complex, and strategically adrift. When Sabia arrived, he needed to sharpen the company's strategy, redesign the supporting structures, processes, and programs, and align leadership priorities and incentives to match his new vision for the company.

When we met him, he told us how he had done all of this but wasn't getting enough behavioral traction to change the customer experience. In short, he was nowhere near where he wanted to be.

Know What You Want

To transform Bell Canada from a monopoly-like conglomerate to a market-focused telecommunications competitor, Sabia knew his employees needed to think and act differently. Their old ways were not going to yield success in this new highly competitive, please-the-customer environment. They needed to learn and adopt new customer-focused behaviors.

According to Sabia, his employees just weren't keeping up. "We've done everything we can think of: we've reshaped our strategy, we've streamlined our processes, and we've launched formal programs to reduce costs and build the new capabilities we need. But far too many of our thirty-five thousand employees aren't changing fast enough. They are like deer in the headlights—confused, frustrated, and anxious. And I can't really blame them."

He confided, "What we've tried so far is taking too long to have an effect. We've made some inroads but we need to move much faster. We can't keep forcing initiatives down our people's throats."

Sabia's problem was typical of those of many large, complex organizations facing the challenge of rapidly changing market conditions. They put in place a new formal organization to address a strategic and operating challenge, yet they are not getting the behavior that the challenge demands.

Despite his love of analytics—he describes himself as a "Cartesian lunatic"—Sabia had an intuitive understanding of the informal organization. He also knew that he had to start with his front line, the people who interacted every day with customers: the retail clerks, the line technicians, the call center operators, and the repair workers. But reaching those thirty thousand–plus employees was daunting. He decided to start with frontline supervisors instead—a mere seven thousand people—because he felt optimistic that, if their attitude underwent a change, it would serve as a tipping point and the masses would soon follow suit. He decided to focus first on the supervisors in customer-facing operations.

Sabia was not only clear about who he wanted to target but also what he wanted them to do. He had evidence that customer satisfaction correlated with employee engagement. He needed these managers to motivate the customer-facing frontline staff to take more pride in the results of their day-to-day work on customer satisfaction.

Learn from Your Best

Despite his frustrations, Sabia had actually seen some progress. In fact, the most recent employee survey contained encouraging findings, ones that many other leaders would have been satisfied with, and Sabia could see that some people were catching on. We asked to talk to some of them.

Sabia arranged for us to meet with Tony Kwok and a dozen other frontline supervisors who excelled at motivating their teams. Their roles ranged from leading call centers to developing new applications for technology. While they had varying tenures with the company, most were battle-tested veterans. All of them were known to be good at taking on tough assignments, but not necessarily "fast tracking" up the corporate ladder. Yet no one doubted their value to the organization.

After spending time with Kwok and his cohorts, we identified five common behaviors that set them apart from most "good managers":

- *Know your people*—create meaningful connections to get to know your team personally and understand individual definitions of success.
- *Recognize success*—use spontaneous pats on the back for the "how" in addition to the "what"; the journey is as important as the destination.
- *Maintain the course*—translate Bell's strategies into local context; prioritize a few goals and follow them; help people stay on track.
- *Use facts to make decisions*—employ a transparent and data-driven process to make hard choices, and always explain the "why" in clear terms.
- *Broaden the work*—create stretch opportunities for everyone based on their skills and goals that go beyond the job description.

Simple stuff, but different from what most managers do. Excited about our findings, we presented them to Sabia's leadership team. There were a few smirks and knowing glances. One executive asked us, "This is what you found? It's all so obvious!"

Perhaps, but then why do so few managers act on those insights? The behaviors were easy to understand and should've been a no-brainer for all the managers. Yet, aside from Tony Kwok and the dozen others, very few managers were actually demonstrating them day in and day out. Apparently, as with eating healthful food and exercising regularly, the remedy was easy to commit to, hard to actually do. Moreover, very few leadership training and development programs talk about the power of fostering pride in the work itself.

Michael Sabia wasn't as skeptical as the rest of his top team, but he wasn't fully satisfied either. "These are exactly the behaviors we need," he told us. "It's great that you found this first dozen. Now we need at least a thousand more exactly like them. How do we do that?" Like good consultants, we nodded knowingly. Then we stepped out of the room and gulped.

Build It, and They Will Come

Since we knew the *what* but not the *how,* we went back to Tony Kwok and the others for help. In the summer of 2004, we gathered them in a meeting room. For most of them, it was the first time they were meeting face to face. We explained what we thought they did differently, and how Michael Sabia wanted us to find a way to quickly develop a thousand more like them. At first they were a bit wary. After all, no one had ever indicated an interest in cloning them. We continued to tell them about how we hoped to codify their behaviors and embed them into training programs and employee manuals. More skeptical looks.

After an excruciating morning, with little to no enthusiasm from the group, we took a welcome lunch break. Over sandwiches and sodas, Tony Kwok and his cohort transformed into different people. They joked and laughed. We heard them exchange war stories about trying to manage at the new Bell Canada. More than once, we heard someone say, "I never thought of that!" Clearly, they were energized by learning from one another. Sensing the energy, we let the group carry on well beyond lunch.

When we gathered them back together to continue our discussion, they again seemed bored and disengaged. They humored us for a while longer. Finally, a call center supervisor who had barely said a word all morning asked us jokingly, "Didn't you take notes at lunch?"

We shook our heads, answering her more literally than she had meant. "That's how we learn—from one another!" she said. Everyone in the room nodded in agreement.

That's when we realized how we could melt through the frozen tundra that Sabia had talked about. We didn't need structured programs, budgets, executive approval, and new role definitions. We could gain momentum simply by finding other like-minded and mutually respectful people and getting them together to share experiences and learn from one another. We could create a community that would attract other like-minded people and then, as it grew, attract the curious-minded.

Over the next few months, we relied on our original dozen motivators to help us identify more. In September of 2004, we and our client colleagues brought together forty people in an unstructured meeting. Our purpose was to give them ample room and "safe space" to talk, exchange ideas, and share stories. Most important, though, we wanted them to interact with Michael Sabia himself about what he could do to find, develop, and clone more of them.

With Sabia listening politely but actively, people began to offer careful and guarded suggestions. Someone cracked a joke and people nervously laughed. We cringed in the corner afraid that the high-energy group we had described to Sabia had just been a dream. But gradually and collectively they became less guarded.

Pretty soon one brave soul sitting next to Sabia pointed out that the directive from the top didn't align with what mattered to the customers. Then another pointed out that the folks in the middle were overloading the system with activities that did not affect customers. With the elephant in the room identified, the ideas and discussion started to flow. They talked about how other elements of the organization were unintentionally misaligned and promoting the wrong kind of behavior. Michael Sabia's positive response to this group rewarded the initial risk involved in such a frank discussion, and the success helped it become an ongoing and valuable activity for this community.

The group left the session with a level of commitment they didn't have when they had come in. Over the next few weeks, they worked together in different groupings as hands-on problem solvers. They morphed into zealots intent on helping Sabia figure out why other frontline managers were not motivating effectively and what aspects of the formal organization needed to change. Sabia told us he didn't need to follow external generic best practices to guide the right behaviors, especially with these motivators already doing what it takes. They were demonstrating the behavior in observable ways, had the language to explain it in ways that resonated with their peers, and thus were starting to trigger change among the people in their networks.

Once Sabia understood what these master motivators were doing differently, the question was how to get many more managers to do it. It seemed obvious to him that if he could get a critical mass of managers across the company to unite, share positive experiences, and focus on similar motivational elements, that could make the critical difference—and he turned out to be dead right.

But first he had to be careful not to get too involved. While his support and commitment were critical, the approach could not be driven from the top. As Sabia's close adviser and chief people officer Leo Houle put it, "The moment we get too far in front of this movement, we'll kill it. We have to learn to learn from our best and be willing to follow their lead."

In the early stages, this small network grew by word of mouth and became a symbol of the change Bell Canada needed. Eventually the informal network became a virtual community that got too big to manage itself, so it put in place some formal roles supported by the corporate center and a limited budget. It developed a few simple processes to bring on new members, plan conferences, and develop local chapters. To make a long story short, in just under two years, more than two thousand members (all of them potential motivators) joined the group, making it the largest community of practice at Bell Canada.

And while the movement to build pride in the work was not the only aspect of the Bell culture change effort, it was the primary source of change energy across the front line.

PROVING THE MOVEMENT WORKS

As the community grew and extended its tentacles across the organization, its impact became increasingly obvious to everyone watching. Yet some wanted to be sure the community was not just a symbol. Mary Anne Elliott, a newly hired SVP of People and Culture, was charged with keeping a finger on the pulse of the movement. She was the one to add formal support when it needed it and to carefully integrate the components into a broader effort to change the culture.

In the early days, Elliott assessed the value of the pride movement by its organic growth—if people felt it was a good use of their already stretched time, it must be adding value. However, she recognized that to convince many of Bell's senior leaders, and to build similar enthusiasm for pride among them, she would need more tangible proof of results.

So she set out to prove that the energy of the informal community and growing sense of employee pride had measurable impact on company performance. Elliott got some unexpected and invaluable help from Karen Sheriff, the president of Small and Medium Businesses (SMB).

Convincing the Skeptics

Karen Sheriff had been trying for some time to improve customer service through increased emphasis on formal training and new metrics. Not satisfied with the results, she turned to her exceptional customer service representatives (CSRs) to understand what they were already doing. They had discovered informal ways to connect to customers and circumvent inflexible rules. They established their own workaround solutions to computer system challenges and went above and beyond what was required to solve customer issues. They were exemplary at providing customer service in the same way that the motivators were exemplary at motivating their teams.

Sheriff wanted to figure out how to spread these behaviors to a larger test group, and to see if following these behavior changes resulted in improved performance. Her team started by developing a list of ten specific exemplar behaviors based on detailed observations of what the exemplars were doing (and not just what they said they were doing). For example, one of her high-performing CSRs was helping a customer whose service was being reactivated after non-payment. The standard process was for service to be restored three days after payment. However, the customer was desperate. He was finalizing a $250,000 contract and needed his accountant to be able to reach him. Much to the customer's relief, the CSR put a temporary message on the line directing callers to the customer's cell phone and also promised to look into expediting the reactivation. Based on this experience, Sheriff added "develop alternatives and always offer something" to her list of exemplar behaviors.

She then organized a series of training sessions focused on the exemplar behaviors for pilot groups of average-performing reps. All the while, she monitored customer satisfaction and call completion in both the pilot and control groups. The pilot groups were taught the exemplary behaviors, but they were also encouraged to work together as peers and share tips and tricks to come up with their own solutions. At the same time they were given more freedom to stray from a script or to satisfy the customer even if it meant taking extra time.

They also tapped into the pride-builder behaviors to help motivate the exemplar behaviors. This became the critical connection between pride and performance.

The SMB pilot was a remarkable success. The reps from the pilot groups outperformed the control groups and received outstanding customer feedback. One pilot center saw a whopping 23 percent increase in overall customer satisfaction over the control group, while another pilot team saw an 11 percent improvement in first call resolution over the control. Bell's leaders were so convinced by the results that they launched a pride-focused training program across the business unit and in other business units as well.

Early on it became clear that change efforts at the front line were working much better than the efforts at executive levels were. Instead of executing harder with the senior group, Sabia decided to focus primarily on where the change was welcome. For the more skeptical executives, he would wait until he had the necessary tools. He reasoned that the experience of joining a conference of hundreds of excited motivators sharing stories and learning from each other would be compelling. And if it wasn't compelling enough, he now had the pilot results as well. Slowly but surely executives joined the movement until a community among themselves formed—the Executive Working Group—to become change agents for the larger culture change initiative. This informal group was connected to the Pride-Builder Community of Practice, and together they helped melt through the tundra.

THE OUTCOME AT BELL CANADA

Michael Sabia and his teams set the stage for one of the biggest cultural transformations in Bell Canada's 120-year history. He created a

powerful network of pride-builders that morphed into a self-energiz-
ing and informal community of pride-builders (nearly two thousand
strong!). These pride-builders drove incredible business performance
and transformed the way thirty-five thousand employees viewed the
business and their role in it.

Bell Canada is an unusual story, and its success was in large
part a function of Michael Sabia's relentless determination. He had
to reach around and through a deeply ingrained culture because
he simply could not wait any longer for change to happen there.
The company has been on a wild ride since our time there. Two
years later, a deal was made to sell the company to a consortium
of investors that included a major shareholder of Bell Canada. The
deal specified a very high share price, largely because of the culture
change results. Sabia left the company and a year later the deal fell
apart. Bell Canada refocused its strategy under new leadership and
built on the culture change effort to continue its transformation into
a more customer-focused company.

DRILLING THROUGH THE PERMAFROST

A similar and perhaps more aggressive mobilization of the informal
played out halfway around the world. India is hardly a country that
needs to worry about any frozen tundra in the physical landscape.
But, Indian CEOs find they still need to worry about that middle
zone of managers who can get frozen into a kind of managerial per-
mafrost that can make employees lower down on the hierarchical
pyramid sluggish and unable to move quickly.

HCL Technologies (HCLT), a global IT services company, successfully transformed this layer of middle management and, as a
result, engineered an impressive turnaround for itself. HCLT, which
employs over fifty-five thousand people and operates in twenty-six

countries, was long thought of as one of India's most innovative IT outsourcers. But when its current CEO, Vineet Nayar, took over in 2005, it was struggling to keep up with the top four performers in its sector.

Nayar recognized that there were many formal elements that were in the way of the frontline employees' ability to create value. So Nayar began by instituting a change program called "Employees First, Customers Second." This philosophy focused on what Nayar calls the "value zone"—the interface between the organization and the customer, where real value is created. Nayar decided that the best way to improve customer service was to put the organization in service to the value zone. To determine the best ways to do this, Nayar collaborated with a group of employees that he called transformers. These people, along with their teams, worked to remove the formal barriers that prevented employees from doing their best work.

The transformers not only developed a variety of informal and formal mechanisms that increased transparency and built organizational trust, they also "turned the pyramid upside down," by introducing the concept of reverse accountability—making functional managers and managers of the enabling functions (human resources, IT, and so on) accountable to frontline employees, not the other way around. In addition, Nayar opened up the performance review process so that the people in the value zone had the opportunity to review any manager who had an influence on them whether or not that manager had direct authority over them.

"Putting employees first isn't about launching a few initiatives that make them feel good," Nayar said in a *Harvard Business Review* article. "It's about offering a workplace where employees, no matter their level, can have an impact, can be a part of something exciting, and can grow professionally and personally."[1] By leveraging the energy of the transformers, Nayar was able to energize employees to take greater pride in their work, specifically in the way they served customers.

As a result, HCLT's customer service performance improved dramatically. Between 2006 and 2008, the company won several major contracts against the global giants. In December 2008, HCL Technologies acquired Axon Group, a medium-sized IT consulting firm. The acquisition has poised HCLT to compete with giants IBM, Accenture, and EDS.[2] In 2008, Hewitt Associates rated HCLT tops on its Best Employer in India list. The same year *Business Week* ranked HCLT as one of the twenty most influential companies in the world.

●　●　●　●　●　●　●　●　●

Of course, the so-called frozen tundra is not really frozen. It is just strongly resistant to top-down, formal approaches that prescribe behaviors and demand execution, leaving little room for individual initiative, responsiveness, and emotional commitment to emerge. Thus it is hardly surprising that it unfreezes quickly when the informal organization activates peer-to-peer interactions and informal networks that connect emotionally to shared values and individual sources of pride.

9

Mobilizing
A Different Kind of Managing

As you know by now, the role of the informal organization cannot be left to chance. The mistake that too many leaders make, however, is trying to manage the informal by applying the same best practices that work for the formal. They find it almost irresistible to create a hierarchy, a program, and a reporting structure for the informal. They put someone in charge of designing a network program, assign someone else to manage it, and have both report to a vice president of the community. These formal leaders proceed to set goals and accountabilities for interactions and launch informal programs defined by critical path milestones, with sharply defined gating factors. Some may pay bonuses to the best networkers. In other words, they shift the informal toward the formal—why would that not work?

Unfortunately, such best practice formal managerial techniques don't work when you need the support of the spontaneous, unpredictable, and ever-changing informal organization. It does not respond well to formal power nor heed defined authority. Because management is largely about bringing order, consistency, and predictability to complex situations, attempts at best practice formal management of the informal will actually squash what is so great about it: its flexibility, spontaneity, initiative, and emotion. You can neither punish nor pay to get informal support—it is an emotional challenge that resists rational methods.

However, that does not mean that leaders at all levels of the organization cannot proactively influence the informal organization to get more traction where they need it. They just need to do so differently. Instead of managing, we think the term *mobilizing* is more descriptive of what is needed—and it highlights the important distinctions.

Of course, *mobilize* has military connotations, typically defined as "marshaling resources for action." When we use the phrase, however, we mean putting human resources in motion that allow the organization to realize the full potential of the ideas and actions of more people. Leaders need to prod the informal organization, to guide or herd it in the right direction without trying to control or constrain it.

Of course, the balance between how much effort a leader puts into mobilizing the informal as opposed to managing the formal is difficult to strike. Most leaders tend to pay attention to one of the two, only to realize they need to compensate by paying closer attention to the other. As at Bell Canada, Michael Sabia turned to the informal only when he realized that formal mechanisms weren't working fast enough. He did not, however, abandon the formal elements in favor of the informal; rather he found ways to get the best out of both.

We believe strongly that the most effective approach, especially at times when leaders need massive change, is to take advantage of both *at the same time*. The amazing story of how a languishing Aetna survived near financial disaster—one of the largest corporate turnarounds in our lifetimes—is an excellent illustration of this integration of the two styles of managing.

Aetna's Turnaround

When the Aetna turnaround story was told in the business press, writers typically focused on the familiar formal elements. They described the strategy reformulation, changes in top leadership, organizational restructuring, cost and headcount reduction, balance sheet strengthening, budgetary control, and operating excellence. This was appropriate because these were all critical elements in Aetna's turnaround success.

However, there is much more to the Aetna story. As comprehensive and impressive as the formal efforts were, they would not have been nearly as effective or efficient without the accompanying informal efforts to transform the organization's culture. With large formal changes demanding their attention, Aetna's senior leaders could easily have focused mostly on the formal programs and left the informal to instinct and chance.

Instead, they worked on both dimensions simultaneously— and by so doing they ensured and accelerated the ultimate dramatic change in company performance. While Bell Canada was a transformation in which the formal and informal changes were initially separated and later integrated, the Aetna turnaround was integrated from the start. For Aetna, it wasn't just about performance, it was about survival.

So the full story—not the one that's been told over and over— starts not in Aetna's massive Colonial Revival building in Hartford but in a restaurant on Manhattan's Upper East Side. Bill Donaldson, then chairman and interim CEO of Aetna, had invited Jack Rowe, CEO of Mt. Sinai/New York University Medical Center (MS/NYU) to dinner. As Rowe recalls, he thought that the purpose of the dinner was to give him a chance to vent to Donaldson about Aetna's performance. Rowe was so dissatisfied with how poorly his institution's claims were being handled by Aetna, he was planning to tell Donaldson that the MS/NYU Medical Center was on the verge of filing a lawsuit against Aetna.

That is not at all how the conversation went. Before Rowe could bring up the claims issue or even hint at the possibility of a lawsuit, Donaldson surprised him. He asked Rowe if he would consider leaving MS/NYU and taking over as CEO of Aetna.

Let's be clear about what Donaldson was asking Rowe to take on: Aetna was near financial collapse. Performance and morale were at an all-time low. The health care industry was struggling with escalating costs, failing government programs, rampant political posturing, and increasingly flawed HMO approaches. By early 2002, the company was losing money at the rate of $1 million per day. As a result, Donaldson, who had been named interim CEO by Aetna's board, was intent on finding his replacement—if not desperate to do so.

Rowe says that he was probably the last person most people would have picked to spearhead a large corporate turnaround. He was a highly respected physician, and had led important medical institutions, including Harvard's geriatric medicine program and the collection of five hospitals and two medical schools that made up MS/NYU. Yet he had no commercial corporate leadership experience or formal business training.

Donaldson didn't care that Rowe had more passion than credentials. In fact, it's probably what made him think about Rowe in the first place. To make a long dinner conversation short, Rowe accepted the offer.

Donaldson's leap of faith paid off. Within five short years, with Rowe at the helm, Aetna rose like a phoenix from the ashes of near-bankruptcy to increase its return to shareholders by over 700 percent. It turned its $1 million per day loss into a profit of over $5 million per day. In 2006, when Rowe turned his CEO role over to Ron Williams, his COO and executive partner in the turnaround effort, Aetna was widely heralded as one of the most successful turnarounds in recent North American history.

First, Identify the Obstacles

When Rowe arrived on the scene as new CEO in 2000, most of the Aetna organization was confused, discouraged, and anxious about its very uncertain future. The employees had been buffeted, battered, and beaten for nearly five years.[1] Rowe knew he faced a massive challenge that went well beyond strategic, operating, and financial revival. And he realized he would need to deal with broad-based emotional and cultural resistance. He quickly identified the factors most likely to prevent him from executing even the most well-intentioned and well-articulated strategy, namely:

A splintered identity. Historically, the "Mother Aetna" culture had taken care of its people no matter what. Reductions in head-count were unheard of—most employees assumed that they were Aetna lifers. However, Rowe and Williams had instituted what they called the "efficient, economic, and hard-nosed" management systems necessary to guarantee financial results. Many people struggled to adjust to these systems and felt the Aetna they had known, the one they had committed to, was a thing of the past. In addition, because of previous acquisitions and divestitures, Aetna was no longer characterized by a single culture. Instead there were several cultural groups with different priorities, behaviors, and values, further fragmenting the Mother Aetna culture.

Loss of motivation. Over the preceding five years, unrelenting negative publicity had been heaped on the company. This was a problem everywhere in the industry: sponsors, patients, brokers, and members believed they were being taken advantage of, if not cheated, by insurance providers. Aetna's name topped the list of villains. Its employees' security was threatened and their pride in their work was eroded. They used to feel good about working on and selling the company's products and services. They had also been proud of Aetna's loyalty to its employees and members. Now, they weren't sure what Aetna stood for, how long the company would last, and whether they wanted to be a part of it. In this unstable environment, job security became the primary motivational focus. People simply hunkered down in hopes of keeping their jobs until the storm subsided or something changed. Rowe knew he needed to find ways to get people feeling good about Aetna again and about their individual roles in the turnaround.

Changing leaders at the top. Prior to Donaldson's ascension, the company had gone through three separate CEO and senior leadership configurations in just a few years. Each new executive established new strategic mandates, operational imperatives, and rules of engagement. One of them, Steve Miller, a recognized master at managing turnarounds, had commissioned six separate and full-time task forces to take apart different functions of the business to drive change management and make improvements. As a result, most employees no longer knew which way was up. But Rowe still had more changes to make. Simply put, the rational change management efforts of his predecessors had had little impact on the deeply rooted and emotional elements of the Mother Aetna culture.

Rowe knew he ran the risk of adding to the confusion, anxiety, and stagnation that often accompanies turnaround urgency. Somehow, he had to figure out how to avoid these pitfalls while gaining some emotional traction and motivating behavioral as well as procedural change.

Formal Councils Designed with the Informal in Mind

Rowe began by energizing networks across the formal process mechanisms.[2] He started with structures such as his standing committees—

the Executive Committee, Management Committee, and Operating Committee. This was a logical place to start because these committees were already focused on governance activities.

But Rowe realized that the formal mechanisms could do little to overcome the emotional and cultural resistance he faced. He needed informal—mostly cross-organizational—mechanisms such as interim councils, forums, and peer networks that would mobilize Aetna's people to believe in and support the change. Hoping to tap into existing networks, Rowe established two rather unusual interim councils:

The Strategy Council. As important as it was to get Aetna's turnaround strategy right, Rowe knew that at the same time he would have to build emotional commitment to the new strategy with the right people at multiple levels in many parts of the company. To that end, Rowe created an unorthodox group he called the Strategy Council. Rather than emphasizing strategic experience or analytical capability, members were chosen for diversity, credibility, and informal influence. In other words, he chose members with high OQ who were adept in two areas: creating emotional commitment among their subordinates, and building strong informal support among their colleagues.

These council members became evangelists for the change. They were sought out as trustworthy sources of information and they promoted the strategic changes through informal interactions with peers in their business areas. Because Rowe and his team had chosen the members so carefully, he knew they would work hard to mobilize people in their respective functions or departments around the changes needed, building confidence and commitment across the company.

The Organizational Effectiveness Council. The Organizational Effectiveness Council was even more unusual than the Strategy Council.

It was similar in its focused purpose, credible and diverse member-ship, and flexible approach, but its challenge was more varied. Its members morphed into various subcommittees and activated infor-mal networks that were able to influence critical pieces of the turn-around effort: organization design, broad-based motivation, and people development.

Normally, these issues would have been in HR's jurisdiction. However, Rowe realized that while HR expertise was helpful, gain-ing traction throughout the organization on these essential top-ics was far more critical. By finding ways to connect peers and use people from across the organization to solve these issues, he would simultaneously be creating pockets of support throughout the orga-nization and getting buy-in before formal changes were introduced.

Again he staffed this council with people who were well respected and connected and encouraged them to reach out to others to gain their perspectives. By connecting these individuals and lending senior support, Rowe and Williams were able to tap into a large set of infor-mal communities all over Aetna. Those networks were highly effec-tive in sharing values, building commitment, and in forming the new Aetna identity.

Although the purpose of these interim councils was sharply focused, their membership and working approach were more flex-ible. As a result they fueled informal networks, relationships, and collaborations, all of which played a critical role in restoring the Aetna identity, motivating emotional commitment, and mitigating the negative effects of repeated changes in senior leadership.

The Path to "The Aetna Way"

Rowe knew that because of Aetna's evolving culture, people no lon-ger had a set of clear values to believe in. In fact, he uncovered at least a dozen different formal value statements that previous leaders had invoked at one time or another over past decades. It would have been easy for Rowe to create an amalgamation or synthesis of those earlier statements—or to craft a new set of his own based on his vision for the company. But Rowe knew that a top-down promulgation of values, no matter how well crafted, would not work in the change-weary organization.

Instead, Rowe saw an opportunity to change behaviors around a set of real, applicable values while simultaneously getting the buy-in needed to build excitement and momentum around them. He held a series of nonhierarchical gatherings in which employees were challenged to reshape a set of values for the new Aetna. This is analogous to the small sessions that Ed Carolan created at StockPot. At Aetna, however, hundreds of people attended the informal sessions. The discussions were designed to be highly interactive and to encourage open and honest participation. In each session, participants were asked to think critically about how to bring the values to life, especially given the new marketplace realities.

The input from these sessions was then used to create a values statement that culminated in a definitive set of leadership behaviors that should apply at several levels. It became known as "The Aetna Way." The document itself was far less important than the process that produced it. By involving employees at all levels, Rowe encouraged dozens, if not hundreds, of informal discussions and networking opportunities, where employees deepened their own commitment to the new Aetna and shared that pride with others.

The most compelling moment in the early stages of the transformation occurred at a meeting where Rowe, Williams, and their senior team were explaining the new strategy to a group of several hundred Aetna employees. It was a formal presentation that was logical, analytical, and comprehensive. At the conclusion, Rowe took questions from the floor.

A woman who had been with the company for more than twenty years—longer than most of the senior leaders in the room—looked Rowe in the eye. She said, "Dr. Rowe, I really appreciate your taking the time to explain all this. But I'm still confused. Can you tell me what this all means for someone like me?"

The room was quiet as everyone anxiously awaited Rowe's answer. It was the central question for everyone in the room: *all this strategic change is well and good but what does it mean to me?* Rowe hesitated as he mulled over his response.

"Well, I guess it is all about restoring the Aetna Pride," he answered, unaware of how relevant this would feel to everyone in the room.

A very surprised Rowe received a spontaneous standing ovation, and that simple, almost accidental notion—*restoring the pride*—became the motivational theme for Aetna as it navigated its way out of financial doom and into turnaround fame.

LETTING GO AND TRYING TO LEARN

A key difficulty for leaders when they mobilize the informal organization is to recognize that they are not dealing with a *complicated problem,* but rather a *complex system.*[3]

Many complicated problems can be solved with the application of expert knowledge. A homeowner may sense something is wrong with the kitchen sink, but a plumber must analyze the problem and respond with the solution. By contrast, in a complex system, right answers are harder to determine and apply because the system itself is in flux and can change unpredictably as the initial steps of the solution are applied. During the financial crisis in late 2008, Treasury and Federal Reserve officials could only try things that they hoped would work, see how the system changed, then amplify what worked, modify what did not work, or try something else. This kind of situation requires an iterative approach rather than a linear approach. Prototype solutions must be tried, the system's reaction observed, and then lessons drawn.

An anecdote reported by David Snowden and C. F. Kurtz in the *IBM Systems Journal* illustrates this well.[4] As an assignment during their final year at West Point, a group of graduates "were asked to manage the playtime of a kindergarten," he writes. They were not thrown into the task, but were given time to make a plan. So, of course, they did what good strategists do: "They planned; they rationally identified objectives; they determined backup and response plans. They then tried to 'order' children's play based on rational design principles, and, in consequence, achieved chaos."

Having rather handily botched the assignment, the graduates decided to take a different approach. "They then observed what teachers do," Snowden and Kurtz write. They saw that "experienced teachers allow a degree of freedom at the start of the session, then intervene to stabilize desirable patterns and destabilize undesirable ones; and, when they are very clever, they seed the space so that the patterns they want are more likely to emerge."

Essentially, this is what Jack Rowe was doing. While managing the formal organization as a complicated problem, requiring rational analysis as well as a command-and-control style, he was simultaneously mobilizing the informal organization as a complex system, requiring emotional insight as well as a try-learn-adapt style to figure out the solutions along the way.

A Sum Greater Than Its Parts

There is some chance that Aetna's turnaround could have succeeded without Rowe and Williams so adeptly mobilizing the informal.

However, we believe it is a small chance, and it would have been a much longer and tougher road to victory. Moreover, it is clear that the three earlier transitional change efforts had been derailed by the informal elements of the old Mother Aetna culture.

If you are like most leaders, you are not facing Aetna's turnaround urgency. However, you are probably shaping a strategy or trying to implement one in a rapidly changing world. Leaders who know how to mobilize and manage simultaneously save lots of time. They are able to make changes to strategies, structures, and processes that are more likely to stick because they have informal support. And they are better able to accelerate behavior change where it matters most for performance.

If you want your entire organization to improvise frequently and energetically in response to fast-moving change, formal management techniques alone won't get you there. You need help from the informal side as well. Mobilizing the informal organization helps support formal management mechanisms, increasing their chances of success and deepening their long-lasting impact on the organization.

PRINCIPLES FOR MOBILIZING

Unfortunately, there is no proven best way to mobilize the informal. It depends on who you are and where you are. A high degree of improvisation and customization is needed in every situation. However, we can point out a few principles that are generally helpful as people try to mobilize the informal while managing the formal.

Concentrate on the Critical Few

Be crystal clear about a few objectives and behaviors. Being clear about the objective promotes reinforcing performance cycles. And identifying three or four behaviors in different parts of the organization that are most critical to accomplishing the objectives allows prioritization and focus in directing change efforts. This provides a North Star for the organization. It enables leaders at all levels to align the formal elements, discover the gaps, and pinpoint the holes the informal must fill. The analytical mind's desire for a balanced scorecard with multiple metrics seldom translates into behavior change down the line. The trade-offs can become confusing and de-energizing at the front line. While viral spreading requires a significant amount of letting go and not worrying about directing the energy that is released, it is important that the enthusiasm created does not dissipate. Sustained focus on the critical few objectives and behaviors will help prevent random momentum that focuses more on activities than results.

Draw on What Is Already Working

In large organizations, there's always a range of things, both human and structural, that are already working and that can be tapped into. Bell Canada, for example, already had managers who exhibited master motivator or pride-builder behaviors, so a new model wasn't needed. Moreover, most people will take more pride in adopting what was developed from within rather than borrowing best practices from other organizations. This accelerates adoption. Sometimes a prototype helps a lot, because it's impossible to predict from the executive suite exactly how things will work out on the firing line. Jack Rowe would probably never have guessed the reaction he would get with his comments about "restoring the pride," but he quickly moved to amplify the message after he received his standing ovation.

Promote Emotional Energy That Feeds on Itself

Rowe spent time with many different ad hoc groupings of employees not just to learn from them but to energize them for the hard road ahead. Finding opportunities to create tipping points, reinforcing cycles, or chain reactions is critical so that the energy latent in the informal organization can rise up and direct itself without requiring an overwhelming use of resources from the formal organization.

Bell Canada's community of practice organized conferences to share learnings, but much of the emotional energy came from Michael Sabia and other leaders taking the stage and personally sharing how important the work of the motivators was, and then interacting informally with the audience. This fed the energy in the room, created "safe space" for open and frank interaction, encouraged connections, and started peer-to-peer story sharing. After people left the event and returned to their day jobs, they continued this viral spreading among peers, colleagues, and subordinates across the company.

Restructuring Zachry

So far, we've seen how CEOs of major companies have led the mobilization of the informal organization. It's always helpful to have the drive coming from the corner office. However, people at all levels of an organization can play an important role in leading the mobilization. In the following example, it was two mid-level leaders at Zachry who helped mobilize the informal organization to facilitate the restructuring of the company from a single business into two separate business units.

In January 2007, life for the Zachry Group was good. Over its eighty-five-year existence, the privately owned, family-led company had grown and diversified significantly. From its beginnings as a small highway constructor in 1922, it emerged as an international provider of diverse construction services—including engineering, quarrying, and both civil and industrial construction.

After years of enduring the cyclical ups and downs of the industry, second-generation CEO Bartell Zachry—who wanted to continue the family legacy—decided it was time to turn the operational leadership of the company over to his two sons, John and David. While both were very capable emerging leaders, their experience, capabilities, philosophies, and management styles differed. John was a University of Texas–educated MBA with extensive experience in industrial markets. David was a professional engineer and MBA who focused on the civil construction side of the business.

The industrial markets and the heavy construction markets had increasingly diverged, and both had grown. As a result, Bartell Zachry and his sons decided to change the strategic and operating approach of the company by dividing into two separate enterprises. This would enable the company to better take advantage of more opportunities and would also enable it to leverage the experience and philosophical approaches of the two sons. John Zachry would run one organization, consisting of the industrial construction, plant services, and engineering businesses. David Zachry would run the other, including heavy (for example, highways and bridges) and building construction, and the cement and aggregates operations. John, David, and Bartell hypothesized that creating two smaller organizations from the large one would enable greater strategic focus and market responsiveness as well as promote organizational flexibility and cultural diversity. It was by no means an easy decision, but it was a move that all believed was necessary.

Nonetheless, the restructuring constituted a dramatic change that called for months of careful analysis, advance planning, and leadership dialogue at multiple levels. John was intent on doubling in size in five years and promoting the Zachry name. David was intent on preserving and strengthening the entrepreneurial and values-based attributes in the civil construction, cement, and aggregates arenas. Both wanted to preserve the fundamental values that had served the company into the third generation of family leadership.

There were also a number of operational concerns to consider. For example the new companies would be located in different buildings, rather than sharing office space. Many service functions—such as human resources, project controls, and estimating—that had been shared by the two operations would now be split in two. Some community outreach activities would also be separated.

To ensure that they got the change right, Zachry's leadership appointed a two-person Culture Team to focus on the emotional and informal aspects of the change. This team consisted of two widely respected employees, Katie Bright and Keith Byrom—one from each future organization—who were chosen based on their ability to mobilize the informal organization. Both Bright and Byrom were dynamic players in the Zachry informal network—well connected informal hubs (fast zebras)—which made them ideal choices for the Culture Team. They knew many people across the company, had good relationships with peers and subordinates alike, and were trusted and respected by many others.

By mobilizing their informal networks to keep close tabs on employee reactions, they were able to ensure that the restructuring avoided overly negative effects on the informal organization, and that the information they were gathering informally would be integrated into the planning process to help manage the restructuring. This served to strengthen collaboration between members of the two future organizations and helped to link them to the formal planning process.

They had many roles and responsibilities:

Identifying key connectivity issues. Through group discussions, Bright and Byrom determined that there were a critical few softer issues where the degree of separation between people in the two organizations would need to be carefully considered. In many cases, complete and immediate separation was appropriate. In others a less complete or more sequenced separation approach was preferable. Moreover, the connectivity issues would need to be addressed differently by each new organization.

Taking the pulse of employees. John Zachry typically relied on his officer groups to keep him informed of the general sentiment of frontline employees about the restructuring. David has always favored a more direct conversation with his employees. Bright and Byrom were able to take the pulse of the organization more frequently and directly by identifying the top forty hubs of the informal networks and visiting with each individually.

As a result they were able to pass very useful information back to John and David Zachry without compromising the sources. In many cases, John used the information to help shape and finalize his new formal processes, while David used the information to strengthen the shared values and other informal elements of his emerging entrepreneurial culture. Different strokes for different folks to achieve change in a critical few behaviors, and often they drew on what was already working in their adjusted plans.

Interpreting the broader implications of emerging reactions. Because of their years of experience within the legacy Zachry culture and with people throughout the company, Bright and Byrom were invaluable interpreters of the different reactions they received from different people in different places. For example, they were able to identify emerging pockets of anxiety within the Equipment department and guide the Zachrys in providing targeted messaging within that group. They generated invaluable positive emotional energy that helped reverse the negative energy, and that was picked up and spread by others as the Equipment department connected more positively with the rest of the organization.

In addition, each business needed to mobilize its informal organization (differently) to ensure that the formal changes would be as successful as possible. To that end the Culture Team focused on clarifying the critical cultural attributes of Zachry, and considering the cultural change implications of future plans in each case.

Bright and Byrom played important roles in mobilizing the informal organization in support of Zachry's restructuring. Such leaders can be found at work in many large organizations. In major change situations, the key for those in the executive suite is to find ways to enlist the support of these leaders and help them spread their energy, while guiding them to be sure their efforts make sense in the context of the big-picture priorities of the company.

• • • • • • • • •

So mobilizing the informal is different from managing the formal, and it is much more than a semantic difference. The most accomplished leaders at all levels instinctively recognize that difference, and find ways to get the best from both. Moreover, they recognize the critical importance of shifting the balance between the two as changing conditions warrant.

Unfortunately, it is easy to become enamored of a balance point that favors one dimension over the other. Start-up organizations who become addicted to their informality often fail to add important rules of engagement dictated by size and competitive urgency. Well-established organizations who become addicted to their advantages of scale and consistency often lose the responsiveness and flexibility that a complex global marketplace demands.

The same kind of imbalance occurs in individual situations. Some people seem to have a formality gene that makes them overlook the importance of informality. Others become hooked on the informal well beyond the point of practicality and performance need. It is not unusual or bad if you are more comfortable working with one or the other. It does, however, constitute a performance improvement opportunity. The complementary skills of managing and mobilizing are important in any change situation—large or small—and change is always in the air.

10

What to Do

C ase studies and examples can be fascinating and illustrative, but you may very well be asking, How do I actually do this? How can I cultivate and mobilize the informal elements of my organization? How can I find and maintain the right balance point as situations change?

In this chapter, we address these questions first in terms of the common challenges faced by everyone in organizations. Then we take a look through three separate lenses—those of individual contributors, team managers, and organization leaders as they consider what they can do in their own jobs.

Common Performance Challenges

No matter how often we talk about mobilizing the informal and balancing it with the formal, we have yet to see that topic appear on anyone's to-do list. That's because mobilizing the informal is a means to the end of solving performance challenges—and it's the latter that worries people. It's important to go beyond the specific examples illustrated thus far and explore a few general performance challenges where we've found insights into the informal organization to be particularly helpful:

- Strategic planning
- Innovation
- Cost-cutting
- Culture change
- Customer service

Strategic Planning

This is the ultimate formal process where analytics, decision making, accountability setting, and plan development rule.

Henry Mintzberg, the well-known professor of management, makes an interesting observation about the typical strategic planning process.[1] He distinguishes between *strategic programming,* which is about *analysis* that involves breaking down goals into discrete strategic plans and activities, and *strategic thinking,* which is about *synthesis* and involves developing a new and integrated perspective based on intuition and visions that are not yet fully defined.

In light of this, Mintzberg recommends that strategy be developed by two kinds of people working together. You need *right-hand planners* for the strategic programming part—people who gather data, conduct analyses, and scrutinize implementation. At the same time, you need *left-hand planners* for the strategic thinking aspect— people who find ideas in unexplored corners of the enterprise, encourage others to think strategically, and conduct rapid prototyping studies. A balance of formal and informal, if you will.

Yet most strategic planning is still dominated by the right-handers of the formal organization. Strategies supported by analytics seem to have much more "truth" associated with them than strategies based on hunches or gut feelings. To a large degree the management consulting profession has reinforced this mindset. Carefully coordinated meetings, standard templates, analytical frameworks, and consistent data all lead to logically compelling arguments. When laid out in dense documents and PowerPoint presentations, such arguments somehow feel more "right" than the most exciting and energizing idea quickly scribbled on a napkin.

One of our clients, T-Mobile, took a different path when formulating its retail concept. Yes, its people gathered data and conducted best-practices benchmarking to develop many useful insights, but they also wanted to ensure that creative ideas were part of the process. So our team met with the retail store associates who were best known for providing customer service, discovered what made them most effective, and created a comic book (yes, a comic book) illustrating the difference between good and great customer service. It also illustrated some realistic and wide-ranging ideas of store concepts that could enable more great service. This informal comic book and formal analyses were all inputs to productive strategy-setting offsites.

An approach to try: Balance formal strategic planning processes with unstructured input from different parts of the organization (recall Jack Rowe's interim strategy council at Aetna), and allow people the time to wallow around in all the information to synthesize new insights.

Innovation

We often ask a simple question when helping clients with innovation: *Are you killing enough ideas?*[2] We believe that is often the best sign of a strong innovation system.

Lots of attention has been paid to fostering creativity and setting up processes that will lead to popular product designs. There is, however, another dimension to innovation that we define as something beyond the creation of neat prototypes: the ability to take a high-potential idea, develop it, and put it out into the market. So innovation isn't just about having a great design or R&D function, it's also about coordinating engineering, IT systems, manufacturing, supply chains, and customer service functions as well.

This is the heart of the challenge. How do you integrate the informal *creative* capabilities with the formal *production* capabilities to get sustainable innovation?

In the best-performing innovation systems we've seen, the most telling indicator of success is that the organization is constantly killing bad ideas and providing resources to the best ones to accelerate their launch. To do so requires a few important capabilities. The common ones are multiple sources of ideas that aren't separated into bad and good too soon, a gradual process of developing and assessing ideas, and decision mechanisms that allow for some ideas to be killed to focus attention and resources on the better ideas. But many uncommon capabilities are also required:

- A sense of pride among idea advocates in the collective journey they take to reach the best decision for the overall idea portfolio at each stage of the process, not just when their idea is successfully and finally advanced.
- Input from all the functions involved in ideas systems—from R&D to customer service—into formal decision processes. These need to be supported by informal team norms that allow for robust debates and good decisions, combining willingness to defend ideas with willingness to accept ideas based on their quality, without regard to who came up with them.
- And finally, effective management of idea shutdowns. Informally, people whose ideas are killed must not be made to feel like failures, either in informal recognition (or denigration) or in formal performance management. And resources should be quickly redeployed to ideas with better potential.

If an organization is killing ideas effectively, it's often a sign that most of these capabilities are in place. You would not be happily and deliberately killing ideas if you didn't have a good integration between the informal and formal capabilities. Note the phrase "happily and deliberately." Plenty of informal organizations kill ideas through a thousand cuts, and plenty of formal organizations make the bureaucracy an idea assassin. Those kinds of kills are not deliberate or helpful.

An approach to try: Create a very visible and central innovation process in which undeveloped ideas can easily find their way to the front end. Integrate informal and formal mechanisms throughout the process (team decision making, communications, sources of pride, metrics) to achieve a desirable kill rate throughout the system.

Cutting Costs

Companies often take an approach to cost cutting that resembles a crash diet. We advocate lean cuisine because it is a healthier and more enjoyable approach, and it helps keep the weight off longer. Unfortunately, few cost-cutting programs succeed in creating long-lasting change. A recent study reports that only 10 percent of companies sustain cost reductions after three years.[3]

Cost-cutting efforts tend to result in a vicious cycle. Formal initiatives are launched to identify cost savings. They reduce headcount, yet productivity doesn't improve. Important capabilities are crippled in ways that weren't foreseen in the original plan. Performance drops. Expenses rise to close the performance gap, and hiring of expensive vendors and contractors negate the headcount savings. Finally, headcount is added back, and the organization returns to its high-cost ways.

Much of this happens because the informal organization was not on board with the mandates decreed by the formal organization. When cost-cutting imperatives are decided behind closed doors, and then commanded top-down, employees are left feeling anxious, angry, confused, and unmotivated. They band together informally to resist the implementation of the cuts. Headcount reductions always test values, erode sources of pride, and damage networks in ways that cannot be countered by the analytic savings templates used to drive these efforts.

This does not mean to say that costs, particularly headcount, should not be reduced. But cuts need to be done in a way that better incorporates the informal organization. By mobilizing instead of mandating cost reductions, surprising results can be achieved.

For example, the Texas Commerce Bank reframed its cost-savings objective from a formal goal as defined by a dollar amount ($50 million, which its people were having trouble achieving) to a more energizing theme: eliminating whatever it is that annoys bankers and drives customers crazy. To determine what those things were, the leaders hosted hundreds of focus groups involving almost half of the bank's nine thousand employees. During the sessions, they built peer-to-peer enthusiasm for "eliminating the annoyances" rather than reducing headcount. They eventually exceeded their original $50 million goal by 100 percent.

Tapping into networks to help the organization stay informed and energized during cost-cutting efforts is critical—but not easy. The informal has to come out of hiding in support of the effort. Particularly in headcount reduction efforts, open dialogues in the context of values are important to keeping the survivors motivated. But perhaps most important, instilling good feelings about and taking pride in the behaviors required to keep costs down is the missing ingredient in those cost-saving efforts that eventually die on the vine.

One of our favorite stories comes from a colleague who was working with a company that exemplified the idea of "proud to be thrifty." Our colleague asked an executive assistant for an eraser. She pulled open her drawer, took out an eraser, cut it in two, gave our colleague one half, and put the other half back in the drawer.

An approach to try: Include people in the challenge of cutting costs. Find hubs in the informal networks to advise you on cost-cutting processes that are fair, transparent, timely, and effective. Engage employees in surfacing solutions and instill peer-to-peer "pride in being thrifty" (although cutting erasers in half will probably not be sufficient to meet your targets). Treat those being let go with dignity in a way that aligns with your values, and don't lose sight of keeping the survivors motivated.

Culture Change

Too often, culture change is treated as an afterthought in a comprehensive change management program. The latter is a rational process known to many human resources and organization development professionals that lends itself to well-defined goals, metrics, and programs that can be managed in traditional ways. Unfortunately, in most cases the focus quickly becomes the accomplishment of a set of activities, rather than achievement of the behavioral shifts that indicate the change in culture.

As discussed earlier, culture is a blend of many elements of the informal organization. One of the most important—and overlooked—factors is to bring the culture to life with real and visible examples. The Tony Kwoks, the Lily Woos, and the Henley MacIntyres are not only important symbols, they are teachers who can spread behaviors virally. They are also credible communicators because they "walk the talk." Change management programs will often circulate stories about these cultural exemplars up and down the hierarchy, but they tend to overlook the importance of side-to-side peer interactions. People learn quite a bit from others doing the same job as them, but often have the least time to do so because of the demands to manage up and down the hierarchy.

An approach to try: Find a double handful of key influencers at multiple levels—special individuals who are already exhibiting the behaviors you want. Get their help in initiating peer-to-peer interactions focused on the specific behaviors that need to change. Find ways to expand peer networks into broader informal interactions. Existing communities of common interest can be very helpful, but you probably also want to think about other broad-based ways to create peer-to-peer connections across formal groups and informal communities that already create forums for interaction.

Customer Service

Making customer service more effective can present a conundrum: How do you provide a meaningful interaction with customers that feels particularly tailored to their needs, while replicating this capability across thousands of frontline employees and ensuring consistency to reinforce the brand?

This is exactly the kind of effectiveness versus efficiency trade-off that the integration of formal and informal mechanisms is meant to avoid. Think of the well-known story about the Nordstrom's employee who accepted the return of a tire—even though the store doesn't sell tires. "Accepting Returns on Items, Such as Tires, That We Do Not Actually Sell" was not a section in the company's employee handbook. In fact, Nordstrom has no employee handbook at all. Instead, it has a seventy-five-word statement that says, among a very few other things, "Our number one goal is to provide outstanding customer service." There is only one rule in the statement. "Use your good judgment in all situations. There will be no additional rules."

This approach succeeds through heavy reliance on Nordstrom's very well-developed informal organization. Other organizations may need a few more rules to help their employees. But they need to avoid situations like those that arise in the airline industry, where flight attendants for most airlines follow standard scripts (or play videos) that bounce off the closed ears of passengers—while Southwest's attendants improvise, engage, and cheer up their passengers.

One approach is to create repeatable processes that are simultaneously sources of pride. For example, a client's executive team went on a retail "experience tour." They stopped at a store selling hair styling, skin care, and make-up products. It felt like a spa. An associate came out, holding a tray in both hands, and offered some herbal tea (a brand that was available for sale at the store). Accepting the tea, a member of the client team asked her about this service.

Her eyes lit up and she explained the offering in detail. Holding the tray with both hands, for example, symbolized that the associate was completely committing her time and attention to the customer. And there were a dozen other nuances involved in this process. Sharing the details and meaning of this standard process created a source of pride for the associate, and she was able to draw on it to create a better experience for the customer. This is better than giving store associates a standard script to follow.

Our colleague Traci Entel has developed a concept she calls the "The Empathy Engine." It provides an interesting perspective on the customer service challenge. By putting empathy into action— both at the front lines and as an organizational engine—and by integrating informal values with formal information flows, companies obtain the benefits of informal and meaningful interactions with customers. At the same time they are able to draw on data in formal processes that further assist service by highlighting opportunities for directing resources to better match customer needs—either at the level of a single interaction (such as providing information about the customer in real time) or in how customer service is provided overall.

An approach to try: Ask employees which rules and processes are getting in the way of serving customers, and get rid of them. Create multiple and diverse sources of pride for employees in customer service processes, and be sure to find ways to provide public recognition for accomplishments that are otherwise overlooked by formal scorecards and metrics. Orient multiple levels of management to the reality of customers' lives and their end-to-end experience. Use flows of formal information and informal stories as reminders of the importance of customers, and to monitor the tangible and intangible aspects of customer experience.

INDIVIDUAL CONTRIBUTORS

Most people do well in the work that excites them and where they have the right support—including emotional support. Unfortunately, most jobs are not always exciting and most leaders are better at providing rational support. The benefit of the informal organization comes in situations where you're not particularly energized about the work you have to do, or where the challenge of the assignment overwhelms the knowledge and resources you have at your disposal, and you really need some help in relieving emotional stress. Those situations are commonly overlooked by the formal organization, which presumes that people are mainly motivated by formal metrics and the monetary rewards of the job, and that the resources assigned to the job are sufficient. When this presumption falls short (as it often does), the informal can help people feel good about getting the unexciting and difficult challenges done.

Some advice:

- Take pride in all your work.
- Build your network connections.
- Expand your capabilities.

Take Pride in All Your Work

It's easy to get motivated for the work you like to do. But what about the dry, tedious tasks that can sometimes dominate your day? It's up to you to figure out how to feel positive about that kind of work and take pride in just getting it done.

We can offer an example from our personal experience: management consulting. The profession appears glamorous to some. And, in truth, most of the work is exciting and engaging.

But picture yourself as a bright-eyed employee who joins a management consulting firm fresh from a top school. You are put on a team working with a big retail client involved in a major transformation. The first assignment: write the job description of a store associate.

"Are you kidding me?" you might think. "I strained my brain day and night in school to write a job description? I could knock this off in an hour. What a waste of my talents."

At least, that is how some might think about that particular work. Others, however—just as smart and talented—might think, "Cool! How do I make a one-pager compelling enough to help in attracting, selecting, guiding, and coaching an associate? This could be a linchpin in the whole effort to create a new customer experience—the key strategic differentiator that we're hoping for." This may be a stretch, but some project leaders in consulting are able to position such tasks in this way and a few new associates are naturally self-motivated and genuinely do think like this. They are the ones who deal best with the ups and downs and become the star performers.

Work is what you make of it, after all, and you can—by yourself—find positive ways to think and feel about the task and increase the amount of pride you take in it.

Understand what work you find frustrating but must be done well in order for you to be effective overall. For example, Katz actually takes pride in ending the day with a clean desk and a vacant e-mail file, seeing it as a way to be at the ready for the next day. Sometimes these little things can make you feel good when other things aren't going so well. Find ways to connect tedious work to other goals, interests, or sources of pride. Be aware of your own definitions of success, and try to create as many bridges to that definition as possible. Identify the new behaviors that will help you perform tedious work more effectively, and publicly announce your goals for change to those who can observe and coach you. Their opinion needs to matter. You should want to avoid disappointing them. For example, something as simple as learning to use a new technology can qualify if you tell your colleagues what you are trying to do. You might even get some friendly competition going with others who have a similar interest.

Build Your Network Connections

By now, you are probably thinking about networks and how they can help you perform. What is less obvious is how to strategically build up the value of your personal networks.

Networks remind us of airport connections. If you fly out of LaGuardia, you can easily get anywhere on the Eastern seaboard. Connecting to Washington National doesn't add that many destinations. But flying to Los Angeles opens up the West Coast and Asia. To expand your destination options, connecting with Los Angeles is better than Washington. The same is true when connecting with people.

However, time is precious and it's hard to build and maintain relationships in large networks. So you need to be strategic—identify and prioritize areas of the organization that could be important sources of information and insight but that you don't often come into contact with. In those areas, identify the few people who seem to be knowledgeable, well-regarded, and willing to help others. Also identify individuals who can complement and enrich your work experiences with theirs. Diversity in your networks not only broadens your perspective, it helps make your work environment more interesting.

Identify the two or three really interesting people you wish you knew better. Find ways to connect with those people. Note this isn't about sharing a beer at a company picnic. You need to connect with them deeply enough so that you learn how you can help them, and they learn how they can help you. It has to be a two-way street. That happens best when you do some form of real work together. And be sure to nurture relationships for their own sake. People who transparently build relationships primarily for career advancement can be viewed as overly political, or even worse, manipulative. At the same time, don't be shy about initiating requests for help—relationships get built through a constant give and take between people, and every successful interaction only builds the willingness of both parties to take further risks with each other.

Expand Your Capabilities

Change happens fast. You may suddenly find yourself in a new job requiring new skills and new connections that didn't seem important in your previous role. By constantly experimenting, you may learn more about what interests you and what skills you have that aren't being put to full use.

In creative work, it's almost always important to be connecting seemingly disparate and irrelevant areas of knowledge into useful insights. So while optimizing your activities to your formal role and routines, be a bit random to create a broader set of informal capabilities that may come into use in new situations. Some of these informal capabilities that seem superfluous to your current formal situation can become highly relevant when formal circumstances change. This increases your adaptability and helps you respond to unpredictable shifts.

Volunteer for jobs that are a bit outside your scope, and be diligent about figuring out what you like and don't like about them. Find ways to connect with people randomly or join groups based on an interest that is seemingly irrelevant to your job. The legendary smoker's circle of information shared by people who regularly take cigarette breaks together often creates cross-hierarchy and cross-group connections. At the same time, think of how others may perceive you based on your current role, and find ways to broaden this perception. If you're an engineer who loves designing product features, try your hand at drafting the advertising copy for a new product. It's likely you'll be included in different kinds of networks that way. It's also likely that you will learn something that broadens your engineering perspective. Whether anyone actually uses your design doesn't matter.

MIDDLE MANAGERS

Being in the middle is tough. Your objectives probably require cross-functional collaboration, but you probably don't have enough time or resources under direct control to achieve them. The rewards system motivates some of your people—but not all. Many of your decisions can be overturned at any point by those higher up, placing your plans at constant risk. These shortages of formal authority and resources mean that most cross-functional work is accomplished through the "web of favors" that middle managers draw upon to get things done.

However, in focusing on how to get things accomplished outside their teams, middle managers shouldn't forget about their teams. Most receive plenty of guidance from the formal organization on how to manage people to do their jobs. Unfortunately, they don't get much guidance for helping anyone but the "A players" who are in hot pursuit of formal rewards and promotion—those less influenced by the formal system seem out of reach.

Thus the picture is more complex for middle managers than for individual contributors. So here are a few informal mindsets and interactions that can help those in the middle to balance their formal authority and become more effective:

- Motivate the average performers.
- Expand your footprint outside the lines.
- Make values-based decisions and talk about them with colleagues you respect.

Motivate the Average Performers

Knowing how to deal with both high and low performers is important. Most organizations provide support to managers to help people at both extremes of the performance spectrum. But that usually accounts for no more than 30 percent of the workforce. The neglected 70 percent in between is often where there is the greatest improvement potential.

To help the middle performers, seek to understand individual definitions of success, particularly those that may not align with the formal system of rewards and incentives. Find ways to connect the objectives of the team to people's individual definitions, and help them take pride in accomplishing those objectives. For example, for those with a genuine focus on maintaining work-life balance instead of rapid promotion, congratulate them when they do a good job *and* manage to get home every night to have dinner with the family.

Connect the average performers to the high performers through small projects. By doing real work together, the average performers learn from the high performers and sometimes long-lasting mentoring relationships emerge. But don't try to force mentoring relationships—that rarely works. Making such positive connections can also broaden the role of the high performers to create more personal satisfaction and prepare them for the coaching role that leaders need to play.

Broaden the forms of public recognition to include the accomplishments of the average. These shouldn't feel like consolation prizes. They must be genuine forms of appreciation for the important role of the B players that differs from that of the over-recognized high-potentials. For example, with the solid but not stellar salesperson who will never be in the "President's Circle" of top performers, find ways to recognize improvements rather than total sales.

Expand Your Footprint Outside the Lines

Middle managers are often the ones who are most constrained by the formal organization when it comes to getting things done—and that means they need a presence in the informal that's outsized compared to their formal footprint. If you are "in the muddy middle," you need to cultivate informal connections between your team, your peers, and important people and forums that make relevant decisions. Focusing on where such decisions are made will help prioritize your team's ability to create and influence relationships.

Figure out which rules to bend or break. Often, formal policies are designed to limit the influence that people can have on the formal machinery of the organization. Without acting like a loose cannon, learn to think like a fast zebra who knows where and when to go with the grain, when to cut across it, and when to find ways around it. Give sufficient air cover to your team if you're asking them to step outside the boundaries, and find sponsors who can slip you a get-out-of-jail-free card if you get caught. In addition, attract resources by making others feel energized by their interactions with you and your team. Most people have a surprising amount of discretion in deciding who they want to help. Make sure that if they choose to help you, they are recognized for the outcome, and they feel good doing it. They will then find proactive ways to help you meet your goals.

Make Values-Based Decisions and Talk About Them with Colleagues You Respect

Your colleagues learn from watching the decisions you make, and how you make them. The rational case for a decision is often clear. What's often not clear is what values might have come into play in making a decision, and how.

Identify the decisions where your workmates need to buy into the outcomes for the decision to be executed. These are likely to be the decisions involving follow-up activities that require sustained energy over time, and where there may be competing alternatives for how to spend that energy. Pay special attention to involving people in the process of the decision. That doesn't mean giving everyone a vote, just making sure they understand the way the decision was made.

Walk the talk, and talk the walk. Be sure you live up to the decision as expected, but also talk often about how outcomes of important decisions link back to the considerations—formal and informal—so people can make sense of how values influence decisions, so they can use them too. At the same time, be explicit about the tensions between values that underlie your decisions and actions. Sometimes values come in conflict with one another—not at the extremes, but quite often in the fuzzy middle. For example, in our consulting work we value client impact and people development. Sometimes it is necessary to choose between or modify the optimal development assignment in favor of client needs, and vice versa. If we always make this decision to optimize client needs, our people development value is eroded.

SENIOR LEADERS

You are in the spotlight. What you do gets scrutinized by many people, particularly when it comes to the informal organization. Unfortunately, you're also the one who can screw things up the most. You have more formal power than most in the organization, and it's very tempting to lean on that power as a way to get things done. But you want the informal to be working with your formal, not subverting it. If you rely on the formal and simply leave the informal to follow suit, you will lose the potential of the informal.

However, you want to act as a coordinator and catalyst of the informal, not the leader. You want to accelerate the development of helpful patterns and seed informal capabilities that others can use. The overall balance between formal and informal is your responsibility. You need to monitor it and make sure your organization is both formally efficient and informally energized. You also need to ensure that you cultivate enough fast zebras to navigate when the unpredictable strikes. Formal information will cascade up to you in the form of reports, but the informal is harder to keep track of, particularly when you're sitting in the executive suite.

Most of our suggestions probably run a little against the grain of what you're already doing; that is exactly what we're hoping you take away. If you are not getting outside your comfort zone, you are missing opportunities. Here are the basics we recommend:

- Learn from the front line.
- Tell and retell stories.
- Shape experiments.

Learn from the Front Line

There's no shortage of advice about the value of "walking around." The trick is to create the opportunities where frontline staff can honestly and safely share with you what is working and what is not, without creating risks for themselves or their managers. We will never forget the office-bound executive who, when pressured into walking around more, ended up making himself and everyone else so uncomfortable that his team begged him to stop. To avoid that trap:

Put yourself in your people's shoes. Try to do their jobs for a day and get a real feel for their sources of pride and frustration. Learn what barriers the organization inadvertently puts in their way, and pay close attention to how the exemplars deal with those barriers. Insights from the exemplars on the front line can be invaluable to leaders at the top. Moreover, the time you spend at the front line signifies the importance of their roles.

Initiate forums for open dialogue at many levels of the organization. Create safe spaces where you can hear from informal leaders at the front line on a regular basis and people can bounce ideas off each other. You need unfiltered data. They will be energized by connecting directly with you, and you will be energized by their passion for helping the organization succeed. While some of your managers in the middle may be worried that you are going around them, you can allay those fears by sharing with them the insights you gain.

Adjust your assumptions about how things work at the front line. Take time to think about what really makes the front line effective, and adapt based on what you learn. Your assumptions flow invisibly into many of the formal plans and designs of your organization—the biggest fallacy being that what motivates senior leaders also motivates the frontline staff.

Tell and Retell Stories

Communication among executives relies too heavily on reports, PowerPoint decks, and scorecards. Leaders need to tell stories so that the rest of the organization can remember what's important, and so they can repeat the stories themselves to amplify the message. Remember, it never hurts to retell the good stories, even if you didn't originate them.

Find people who exemplify the behaviors you want to see more of and tell stories about them, showing what people who behave that way do. Pay particular attention to people whose behaviors already represent the way of the future, but who are not receiving the attention from the mechanisms that tend to reward excellence in the present.

Make explicit the informal aspects of what these exemplars do to be so effective by bringing them into the conversation. What values do they bring to life? How are they connecting with others beyond the formal organization? What sources of pride do they draw on, and how do they instill pride in others? What are they doing that most people are not doing?

Get help. Most senior leaders are simply not as good at storytelling as they are at speech-giving. Find someone who does have the storytelling gift to help you shape a story that is memorable, insightful, and personal. Practice it a few times on a friendly listener.

Shape Experiments

The informal organization is always testing the boundaries of the formal. Shortcuts, workarounds, and bypasses help people get work done in ways that the formal cannot help them with. That's natural, because the formal aims for homogeneity whereas the informal encourages individuality. Without disrupting the natural aims of the formal, senior leaders can give implicit permission for tests and pilot programs that can provide useful learning to the rest of the organization—perhaps even the seeds for broad-scale changes to the formal.

Look for potential innovators who achieve high levels of performance in ways that are not typical in the formal organization. They usually invent new routines to complement formal rules. Seek the potential innovators who are also fast zebras and plant them in spots in the organization where their networking skills can catalyze their innovative instincts by involving others.

Give them space to expand their success. Create clear objectives for their experiments and hold them accountable. Make it clear what you're trying to accomplish and how they can accelerate that the process.

Provide the right level of resources to help them along, but not so much so that the experiment is too easy. Make them sweat a bit—that will focus their creativity and make them even more proud of their accomplishments. Don't forget to make them proud of the journey as well as the destination.

ON MONDAY . . .

There is one best way for you to gain the maximum impact from reading this book: take something you have learned and apply it to your own role so that you do something different from what you now do. In other words, change something about yourself before trying to change something about your organization.

At the core, of course, you are who you are, and changing your essential nature is probably impossible—and anyway not really the point. But there are, no doubt, two or three new behaviors that you can adopt that will make better use of the informal organization in your role. Figure out what they are and try one of them next Monday. This next Monday—not at the beginning of the fiscal year, not after the big project is over, and not when you get your next role. After a while, if the first behavior works, try another. And if that first one doesn't work at all, try another one anyway. Eventually, change will come and improved performance will follow.

In Conclusion

At this writing, we are emerging from one of the most severe economic downturns in the past century. People are poking their heads out of the bunkers, hoping to continue business as usual. But the previous ways of working—well, we all know that they just won't work anymore. The world continued to change in these past few years, and we're only starting to see the implications on a global scale. China will soon have the largest number of English speakers of any country in the world. We now generate more information in one year than we have in the past five thousand. Facebook has a population larger than most countries. The number of text messages sent in a year exceeds the number of people on the planet.

Yet much of the human experience remains unchanged. We want to do a good job. We want to be proud of our work. We want to connect with people. We want to live a values-driven life. These powerful forces remain constant in the midst of dramatic social, technical, and ecological change.

To be successful in an increasingly changing world, individuals, leaders, and societies must make better use of these underlying forces. The informal organization is a ubiquitous and constant influence on any group of people working together to achieve common goals. The folk wisdom of the informal is often overshadowed by the professional smarts of the formal. Whether you are Lily Woo trying to improve a school, Tony Kwok energizing his field operations team, Henley MacIntyre getting things done at the UN, or Jack Rowe leading a corporate transformation—the essential factors for motivation, collaboration, innovation, and inspiration remain the same. Different organizations face different challenges—but one human species populates them all.

While the fashion of management theory encourages throwing out the old to make room for the new, that is not what we are proposing. Rather we are urging you to

- Keep and strengthen your formal management approaches— just realize their limitations.
- Avoid viewing the informal organization as unruly chaos—it can be influenced and energized to accelerate performance results and strategic imperatives.
- Refuse to manage the informal with the techniques that work for the formal—you will only make things worse.

When the informal organization is mobilized to balance the formal organization, the overall construct is whole and complete. New levels of performance result. It is like pushing a swing. New heights can only be achieved when the pusher and the swinger are in sync.

We work with all kinds of organizations—some that favor the informal, some more inclined to the formal, and many that are rethinking the balance of the two. In all of them, we are concerned with helping individuals, managers, and leaders achieve higher levels of performance. On one hand, we may have oversimplified this task by breaking the complex world of human organizational behavior into two buckets. On the other hand, however, we are convinced that this bucketing provides a more practical and useful mindset than some of the more complex frameworks for human behavior for leaders who want to drive change rather than study it.

And this book is intended for those leaders. Our many examples and case studies demonstrate some of the complexities involved in getting the best from both the formal and informal organizations, but they also illustrate the many different ways that leaders can achieve integration of the two. It is the mindset, the bias toward balance and integration, that differentiates the peak performers from the also-rans—be they individuals, teams, or enterprises.

As you travel along this road, however, recognize that achieving integration is dynamic—a moving target. All we can offer is a range of ideas, options, approaches, and examples to draw from—only some of which will fit your needs and your organizational DNA.

In addition to the ones we offer here, we know that you will find your own and they will help you be successful in leading outside the lines.

About Our Sources and Methodology

The stories in this book are based on material from a variety of sources. The majority of the stories come from our own experiences, primarily in working with clients. We have used the real names of the people featured in the stories, except where we have indicated that the name has been changed, to protect the privacy of that person. The scenes described are based on actual scenes and the conversations described are based on actual conversations. However, the conversations are recollected from memory, rather than quoted directly from transcripts, so they should not be considered as word-for-word accurate. The people whose conversations are included in the book have reviewed the material for accuracy and we have made adjustments in response to their comments. Some of the stories include additional information gathered from secondary sources; where the information can be attributed to a particular source, we have cited the source in the Notes. A few stories contain general information available through a number of secondary sources, with no specifics gathered from any one source or any direct quotations; these sources have not been cited.

INTRODUCTION

The call center story came from a Katzenbach Partners client in Troy, Michigan. Our colleagues at this particular client were using an approach we call the "exemplar observations" in which we attempt to observe both "exemplar" and "good enough" performers in their work situations to tease out the critical differences. We changed the names of the people involved and some of the details to create an illustrative example.

CHAPTER 1:
THE LOGIC OF THE FORMAL; THE MAGIC OF THE INFORMAL

The backgrounds of Frederick Taylor and Douglas McGregor are well known—we synthesized from multiple sources. Harold Leavitt's story is taken from *Top Down*—we just found the recounting too intriguing to not include it word-for-word. The Caja Navarra story was based on material from numerous sources, including *Leaders,* www.thefinancialbrand.com, and a presentation by Pablo Armendáriz, head of innovation at Caja Navarra.

CHAPTER 2:
WHEN THE BALANCE SHIFTS

We originally studied The Home Depot in the research for *Peak Performance,* which gave us insights into the original informal and formal organizations. Subsequent information about the changes happening at The Home Depot were taken from public sources. We gathered deeper insights from confidential interviews with two former executives, here combined under one pseudonym—"Henry." Chester Barnard's work was a pleasant surprise from an old text. When Katz was in school, Barnard had a reputation as what we would call today a *guru,* but his wisdom has unfortunately faded into the background. The Starbucks story was taken from a previous Katzenbach Partners publication: *The Informal Organization.* Our story on the !Kung was supplemented by several sources. Tempted as we were, we didn't conduct field research among them. The path of changing balance points described in "An Ever-Changing Balance Point" was drawn from our experience serving clients and watching them go through several of the tipping points we describe. The eBay story originally appeared in an article on *The Informal Organization.*

CHAPTER 3:
JUMPING TOGETHER

We often cite Mary Parker Follett's work—it's another example of overlooked wisdom from the past. The story about the president wanting to "bomb that minority right out of here" was actually a president at one of the clients we discuss in more detail elsewhere in the book—we won't say which one. Enron was an "almost" client; Katzenbach Partners examined its employee engagement scores in preparing a proposal (that was not accepted) right before the company imploded. We interviewed several people at Orpheus to better understand their fascinating organization, and we also served them pro bono to help define a strategic planning process that reflected their informal organization. Katzenbach Partners also served the Houston Police Department, and we supplemented our work with interviews conducted especially for this book.

CHAPTER 4:
IT'S ALL ABOUT THE WORK

Our additional findings on the importance of pride in motivating day-to-day work were based on work with several clients after the initial research conducted for the book *Why Pride Matters More Than*

Money. The research on the effect of external rewards on intrinsic motivation is found in many fields; we drew primarily from research conducted in education. Specifically, we found *Intrinsic and Extrinsic Motivation: The Search for Optimal Motivation and Performance,* edited by Carol Sansone and Judith Harackiewicz, to be a useful overview. The characteristics of master motivators were drawn from over a hundred detailed case studies in many organizations where we would ask the master motivators and their teams what made them so unique. While the specific behaviors they demonstrate vary from company to company, overall they could be characterized by these traits. Our story about Ken Mehlman is largely based on interviews with him and members of his team.

CHAPTER 5:
VALUES DRIVEN, NOT VALUES DISPLAYED

The values statements for Enron and the Marines are publicly available. We also had direct experience with both organizations to confirm how they did (or did not) follow their values. Katz's thirty-nine years with McKinsey and close working relationship with Marvin Bower were the source of the well-known "What would Marvin do?" illustration. We originally found Gentle Giant in a *Wall Street Journal* story. Our team visited the company and we interviewed several of its people. In fact, Katz used Gentle Giant for a family move and can attest to their personal service. When things didn't seem to be going right, a few executives showed up on his doorstep to help. Reliant was a long-time and significant client of Katzenbach Partners. We supplemented our client experience with tailored interviews with the cited individuals. The interesting research about the "transmission" of values through networks first came to our attention from the widespread publicity received by the *New England Journal of Medicine* article by Nicholas Christakis and James Fowler. Interestingly, about a hundred people in our personal networks forwarded that article to us.

CHAPTER 6:
IT's STILL ABOUT PERFORMANCE

We first met Ed Carolan in our work with The Campbell Soup Company to help his team think about using the informal organization to enhance what was already strong performance. Subsequent visits helped reveal the truly remarkable way he thought about metrics in helping drive StockPot's performance (among other levers). We first came across Gregg Sheehy's interesting approach at a TeleTech conference where Katz was giving a presentation, and we conducted additional interviews to gather his insights into motivating outside of literal organizational lines. We've had the pleasure of working with Kyle Ewalt for several years—this story was one of many we could have told.

CHAPTER 7:
SETTING THE FAST ZEBRAS FREE

Katzenbach Partners served Mark Wallace at the UN, and we conducted subsequent interviews with him and Henley MacIntyre. We met with Lily Woo on a few occasions, and have to admit that it's still intimidating to sit in the principal's office. The chaotic environment of PS 130 was quite different from that of the NYC Department of Education office, where we met with Eric Nadelstern.

CHAPTER 8:
MELTING THE FROZEN TUNDRA

Katzenbach Partners served Bell Canada over several years, and many of our initial insights were developed by working closely with Michael Sabia, Leo Houle, Mary Anne Elliott, Karen Sheriff, and most important, the Pride Builder Community of Practice. They drove a highly original approach to changing culture to drive higher performance.

CHAPTER 9:
MOBILIZING: A DIFFERENT KIND OF MANAGING

Katzenbach Partners was working with Jack Rowe when he was at Mt. Sinai/New York University Medical Center, and subsequently served him on a range of issues over the course of Aetna's turnaround. The firm also served Zachry over a number of years as it executed its transformation into two companies.

CHAPTER 10:
WHAT TO DO

These recommendations stem from a range of our client experiences, particularly when we apply insights about mobilizing the informal organization directly toward the business challenges we discuss. The Texas Commerce Bank story comes from Katz's work with the bank (as told in *Real Change Leaders*). Interestingly, the client executive he worked with, Anita Ward, was a graduate anthropologist who was one of the key behind-the-scenes architects and movers. Similarly,

the leadership recommendations come from direct client engagements where they are seeking guidance for different leadership roles,
and indirectly from observing talented leaders and offering informal
coaching.

DIAGNOSTIC TOOL

These questions and tests are actual frameworks that we have used
in client engagements, slightly edited to fit the format of the book.

A Diagnostic Tool:
Assessing Your
Organizational Quotient

This tool assesses the ability to draw on both the formal and the informal for high levels of performance. For the purposes of these questions, assume that the organization you're in functions relatively well.

Answer each question on a 1–5 scale:

1 = Who is this?
2 = Not really me
3 = Sort of me
4 = Most of the time me
5 = That's me!

1. I see a connection between my team's sense of what's right and how leaders talk about the organization's values.

2. What I learn from both official communications and water-cooler chatter helps me understand what's going on.

3. When I need a decision, I know where to go and who can help me get the outcome I want.

4. It's clear to me when I should be working with others, what our mutual goals are, and how we should collaborate.

5. When stuck on a problem, I draw upon both the company's tools and my networks to find the knowledge I need to get it solved correctly and quickly.

6. I find a way to feel good about the work I have to do to meet my performance objectives, but don't really like to do naturally.

7. I often hear about lots of good ideas, and find ways to help the best ones get resourced and implemented.

8. When there's general agreement that we need to change, I feel confident that I'll know what to do differently and I'll be able to manage the change personally.

9. I understand and empathize with my customers' needs and feel equipped to meet them.

10. I have many opportunities to learn and try new things without necessarily being promoted.

For those questions where you scored yourself consistently high (a 4 or 5), congratulations—you've got high OQ on an important formal-informal balance. The following paragraphs explain the larger meanings and implications of each question. If you scored yourself a 3 or below on any question, pay special attention to that discussion; you might improve it for yourself or your team.

1. *Values alignment:* How closely do your work group's values align with the organization's values? If the organization's stated values are different from yours but still widely held by others, chances are you're in a bit of a maverick group and you'll need to find ways to connect with others. Outsiders find it hard to connect with your group, and your group will similarly find it difficult to connect with groups outside your own. If the organization's stated values aren't truly held by anyone in any group, then it will be hard for any group to collaborate with any of the others.

2. *Communications channels:* If you're not finding official communications useful, then you're either spending too much time on them or you're not employing them properly. Studies show that high performers are often those who quickly learn what messages they need to delete or ignore. If you're not learning from water-cooler chatter, you're disconnected from important communications chan-

nels. Find a way to connect with people on an informal basis, and then they'll start sharing with you. And if it becomes just gossip—don't dismiss it immediately. Sharing gossip is a way people develop trust with each other.

3. *Decision rights and influencers:* If you don't know where to go for decisions, then you need to spend more time understanding how resources are formally allocated. A low score in this area means that when it comes time for you to make a budget request, you won't know how to steer it through the process. Also, you'll need to know who has influence in the decision-making process so you can rally their support early.

4. *Fluid and structured collaboration:* Working together is both a value and a process. If you find the group experience unpleasant, you may be ignoring some behavioral problems that are the elephant in the room. Find a way to bring them up—everyone else is thinking the same thing. If your group enjoys time with each other but finds it unproductive, then you may need a more formal process of structured agendas, meeting rhythms, and so on. But most likely the biggest problem is the lack of a clear objective. Work with your team to crystallize the problem you're trying to solve and the definition of success for the group's work.

5. *Predictable and unpredictable problem solving:* If you're not using any of the company's tools, chances are that you're reinventing the wheel. Ask others how they solve the problems you find yourself coming across regularly. If you don't know who to go to for out-of-the-ordinary problems—do the same thing. Ask people, and you'll likely hear the same names over and over again. Otherwise, when you interact with people, invest a bit more time to learn what they know and share what you know.

6. *Motivating all the work:* This is important—it affects how you feel for the majority of your waking hours in the week. Other than the suggestions already given in this book, try to find a way to

shape your work tasks with your manager to make them personally more meaningful. If that's not an option, look for ways to work with either colleagues or customers to help you "feel good" about whatever you have to do—their acknowledgment alone is often a source of pride.

7. *Creativity and production:* If you're not hearing about creative ideas, chances are you're not generating creative ideas yourself because you're not in the flow. Ask someone who you should go to for help to brainstorm a creative solution, and establish a relationship with that person. Without a view of which ideas get selected for implementation, you may not have a sense of what the decision makers view as important criteria.

8. *Change capacity:* You'll first need a good understanding of the "from-to" change comparison of the company at large (what the current state of the company is and where it is trying to go), and then your personal "from-to" change. You'll feel confident if you understand the formal tools like training that will be made available, and also how networks and pride-building managers and colleagues can support you.

9. *Customer empathy and responsiveness:* Listening is the first step to really wowing customers. Put yourself in their shoes; imagine their story as they enter the door. But understanding the problem is only half the solution. Make sure you know how to draw on relationships between different functions and groups that touch the start-to-finish customer experience so you can bring resources to bear to solve customer problems. Don't be shy about asking for favors from others when you need help meeting a customer's needs. When the customer is satisfied, be sure to build pride among your colleagues by sharing the success and recognition, particularly with those who are one step removed from the front line.

10. *Personal development:* It's critical to take risks, but to do so requires both formal flexibility in your role and duties and a sup-

porting informal system that reinforces values of growth and explo-
ration. Start by working with your manager. Most people want their
teams to grow, but may not have the time or insight to help them.
By helping your manager help you, you can get one step ahead. If
your manager is resistant, find colleagues who will let you experiment with them in some of their roles that you find interesting.

How to Strike a Better Balance in the Organization

The first of the following sets of questions aims to identify the organizational capabilities that need to improve, and the second assesses the relative strength of the formal and informal elements of your organization. With this knowledge, you can take specific actions to improve performance.

Assessing Organizational Capabilities

On a scale from 1 to 7, with 1 being "Weak" and 7 being "Strong," how would you rate the following capabilities:

1. *Effective decision making:* The capability to identify, analyze, and choose among different courses of action that are then executed. □

2. *Successful innovation:* The capability to recognize significant value-creating opportunities and create solutions to generate unique products and services. □

3. *Superior responsiveness and adaptability:* The capability to draw out implications from marketplace events, translate those into possible changes, and adapt accordingly. □

4. *Cross-organizational collaboration:* The capability of groups and individuals to interact across organizational boundaries and work together productively on the hardest problems that require help from people in different parts of the organization. □

5. *Timely execution:* The capability to complete tasks more rapidly and with less re-work than competitors. □

6. *Constant improvement:* The capability to continuously capture small-scale opportunities for increasing productivity, responsiveness, and quality. □

Assessing the Balance Between Informal and Formal Elements

On a scale from 1 to 7, with 1 being "Weak" and 7 being "Strong," how would you rate the strength of the following elements of your organization:

1. A clear strategy that aligns the decisions made by different functions and units across the organization ☐

2. Values that are visibly demonstrated in the organization and that productively guide and align the actions of individual employees ☐

3. Organizational structures, processes, and programs that make the completion of regular tasks efficient ☐

4. Informal personal networks and relationships that can be drawn upon for communication, work-related knowledge, trusted advice, and energy ☐

5. Individual metrics and goals that are clear in how they reward performance ☐

6. A sense of pride in the work that motivates behavior that yields high performance ☐

Add up your scores for 1, 3, and 5. That's your "formal" strength. Now add up your scores for 2, 4, and 6. That's your "informal" strength. Are they balanced?

Putting It Together

The following table offers some suggestions for improving organizational capabilities, depending on whether the formal or informal is dominant.

Capability	Formal Is Dominant	Informal Is Dominant
1. Decision Making	Ensure decision-making bodies have values and norms that allow for real dissent and debate.	Clarify accountabilities and decision rights of various groups, ensure the right data inputs for decisions, and communicate the outcomes clearly.
2. Innovation	Motivate upstream creativity to generate more ideas.	Instill downstream production discipline to select the best ideas and drive them to development.
3. Responsive adaptation	Use informal communication networks to sense changes—repeat trends will quickly be amplified.	Establish quick decision-making processes and clear accountabilities for action plans that can be activated once trends have emerged.
4. Collaboration	Create cross-functional teams focused on real work that encourages network building.	Clarify processes and workflows to coordinate activities and governance.
5. Execution	Build pride in achieving results instead of just following the rule book.	Create metrics and incentives that clarify who needs to do what and by when.
6. Improvement	Shape values around risk taking and experimentation.	Codify procedures so that changes can be rapidly captured and spread.

Notes

INTRODUCTION

1. We have changed the names of the reps in this story. The conversation is based on several we had over the course of our visit to the call center.

2. Douglas McGregor, "Theory X and Theory Y," *Workforce,* 2002, *81*(1).

CHAPTER ONE

1. Tom Robbins, *Another Roadside Attraction* (New York: Bantam Dell, 1971).

2. Frederick Taylor, *The Principles of Scientific Management* (New York: HarperCollins, 1911).

3. Douglas McGregor, *The Human Side of Enterprise* (New York: McGraw-Hill, 1960).

4. Abraham Maslow, *Motivation and Personality* (2nd edition) (New York: HarperCollins, 1970; originally published 1954).

5. Frederick Herzberg, "One More Time: How Do You Motivate Employees?" *Harvard Business Review,* Sept.-Oct. 1987, *65*(5), 109–120.

6. This discussion draws on the notions of the tyranny of either/ or described by Jim Collins and Jerry Porras in their classic

work, *Built to Last* (New York: Harper Business Essentials, 1994).

7. Harold J. Leavitt, *Top Down* (Boston: Harvard University Press, 2005), p. 63.

8. Daniel Goleman, *Emotional Intelligence* (New York: Bantam, 1995), p. xii.

9. Edward Thorndike, "Intelligence and Its Use," *Harper's Magazine,* 1920, *140,* 227–235.

10. Daniel Goleman, *Working with Emotional Intelligence* (New York: Bantam, 1998), p. 3.

Chapter Two

1. Chris Roush, *Inside Home Depot: How One Company Revolutionized an Industry Through the Relentless Pursuit of Growth* (New York: McGraw-Hill, 1999).

2. Chester I. Barnard, *The Functions of the Executive* (30th Anniversary Edition) (Cambridge, Mass.: Harvard University Press, 1968), p. 8.

3. Anna Muoio, "Growing Smart," *Fast Company,* July 1998; retrieved from www.fastcompany.com/magazine/16/one.html, December 29, 2009.

4. Marshall Goldsmith and Mark Reiter, *What Got You Here Won't Get You There* (New York: Hyperion, 2007).

5. George Anders, "Business Fights Back: eBay Learns to Trust Again," *Fast Company,* December 19, 2007; retrieved from www.fastcompany.com/magazine/53/ebay.html?page=0%2C1, November 17, 2009.

Chapter Three

1. E. O. Wilson, *Consilience: The Unity of Knowledge* (New York: Knopf, 1998).

2. Pauline Graham, *Mary Parker Follett—Prophet of Management: A Celebration of Writings from the 1920s* (Boston: Harvard Business Press, 1995).

3. Karl Weick, "The Sociology of Organizing," 1979 (Rensis Likert Distinguished University Professor at the Ross School of Business at the University of Michigan).

4. Thomas J. DeLong and Vineeta Vijayaraghavan, "Let's Hear It for B Players," *Harvard Business Review HBR OnPoint Enhanced Edition,* June 2003; retrieved from http://hbr.org/product/let-s-hear-it-for-b-players/an/R0306F-PDF-ENG?conversationId=64071, December 29, 2009.

5. Note that quartets and chamber groups typically do not have a conductor.

Chapter Four

1. Jon R. Katzenbach, *Why Pride Matters More Than Money* (New York: Crown Business, 2003).

2. Bob Sutton, "An Astounding Intervention That Stopped Employee Theft," Work Matters, May 14, 2009; retrieved from http://bobsutton.typepad.com/my_weblog/2009/05/an-astounding-intervention-that-stopped-employee-theft.html, November 17, 2009.

3. Leon Festinger, *A Theory of Cognitive Dissonance* (Stanford, Calif.: Stanford University Press, 1957).

4. Carol Sansone and Judith M. Harackiewicz (eds.), *Intrinsic and Extrinsic Motivation: The Search for Optimal Motivation and Performance* (San Diego, Calif.: Academic Press, 2000).

Chapter Five

1. April Goodwin, "Reliant Energy's Clean-Coal Plant," *Constructioneer,* January 19, 2004; retrieved from www. allbusiness.com/print/6287221-1-22eeq.html, November 17, 2009.

2. Clive Thompson, "Are Your Friends Making You Fat?" *New York Times Magazine,* September 13, 2009; retrieved from www.nytimes.com/2009/09/13/magazine/13contagion-t. html?ref=magazine, December 29, 2009.

3. Nicholas A. Christakis and James H. Fowler, "The Spread of Obesity in a Large Social Network over 32 Years," *New England Journal of Medicine,* July 26, 2007, 357, 370–379.

4. "Software That Spots Hidden Networks: Electronic Ties That Bind," *The Economist,* June 25, 2009; retrieved from www.economist.com/businessfinance/displaystory.cfm?story_ id=E1_TPJTVSJR, December 29, 2009.

5. Cataphora, "E-Discovery," n.d.; retrieved from www.cataphora .com/solutions/legal/ediscovery.php, December 17, 2009.

Chapter Six

1. "Want to Talk to the Chief? Book Your Half Hour with Susan Lyne, CEO of Gilt Groupe," *New York Times,* Oct. 3, 2009, Business section, p. 2.

CHAPTER SEVEN

1. Jane Barrer, comment posted to message boards at www
   .greatschools.net, April 30, 2007.

CHAPTER EIGHT

1. Douglas A. Ready, Linda A. Hill, and Jay A. Conger,
   "Winning the Race for Talent in Emerging Markets," *Harvard
   Business Review,* November 2008.

2. Steve Hamm, "HCL's Leveraged Leap to India's Top Tech
   Circle," Information Technology blog on BusinessWeek.com,
   December 15, 2008; retrieved from www.businessweek.com/
   technology/content/dec2008/tc20081214_882277.htm,
   November 17, 2009.

CHAPTER NINE

1. Much of the detail for this account was developed by Roger
   Bolton, EVP at Aetna during the turnaround, for a book he is
   writing with Jon Katzenbach and David Knott, senior partner
   at Booz & Company.

2. Jim Collins and Jerry Porras coined the term "mechanisms"
   in their classic best seller, *Built to Last* (New York: Harper
   Business Essentials, 1994).

3. This is based on David J. Snowden and Mary E. Boone, "A
   Leader's Framework for Decision Making," *Harvard Business
   Review,* November 2007; retrieved from www.mpiweb.org/
   CMS/uploadedFiles/Article%20for%20Marketing%20-%20
   Mary%20Boone.pdf, November 17, 2009.

4. David Snowden and C. F. Kurtz, "The New Dynamics of Strategy: Sense-Making in a Complex and Complicated World," *IBM Systems Journal*, 2003, *42*(3).

Chapter Ten

1. Henry Mintzberg. "The Rise and Fall of Strategic Planning," *Harvard Business Review*, January 1994; retrieved from http://hbr.org/product/fall-and-rise-of-strategic-planning/an/94107-PDF-ENG?Ntt=The+Rise+and+Fall+of+Strategic+Planning, December 29, 2009.

2. Zia Khan and Jon Katzenbach, "Are You Killing Enough Ideas?" *Strategy & Business*, August 27, 2009.

3. Suzanne P. Nimrocks, Robert L. Rosiello, and Oliver Wright, "Managing Overhead Costs," *McKinsey Quarterly*, May 2005; retrieved from http://www.mckinseyquarterly.com/Managing_overhead_costs_1604, December 29, 2009. In addition, much of this material is from Paul Bromfield and Jon Katzenbach's "Energizing Employees in Recessionary Times," white paper, Booz & Company, 2008.

Acknowledgments

There are many to thank for their help in the journey that resulted in this book.

First, we thank the Katzenbach Partners community. The firm not only sponsored our work, it encouraged its many informal networks to provide invaluable insight, stories, and wisdom along the way. Alex Goldsmith was particularly helpful as a sounding board for our early ideas and a window on likely reader reactions. The firm also provided the environment where we were fortunate to meet each other, and where we spent many years working and laughing together and with our incredible colleagues.

While all contributed in some way, a few others stand out in their direct contributions. We were ably assisted by Allison Kean, David Paltiel, and Michael Noon in researching stories and preliminary book outlines. Michael Walker in particular played a key role in coordinating the various research efforts and finding time to support various project management aspects of the book while pursuing his passions in the arts. Abe Tarapani developed the Zachry case study.

We extend our thanks to the clients and collaborators who believed in our ideas, took risks with us, shared their stories, and helped formulate our thinking. At the end of the day, the impact of our ideas is measured by their ability to help leaders at all levels achieve performance improvements. Our "first adopters" paved the way for many others to benefit from what we learned together.

We couldn't have pulled all of this together without the thought-partnership and able writing assistance from John Butman. We also benefited from Charlie de la Fuente's able proofreading.

After the combination of Katzenbach Partners with Booz & Company, we received fresh (and helpful) feedback on our ideas. Art Kleiner, Jonathan Gage, and Tom Stewart helped us think through a marketing strategy, along with Ilona Steffen, as director of the Katzenbach Center at Booz & Company, where the further pursuit and incubation of formal-informal integration continues as a priority focus. Christine Broux and Efram Lebovits helped manage the book project in its last stages.

Our team at Jossey-Bass helped make this book a reality. Karen Murphy understood what we were trying to do and helped us shape our preliminary manuscript into the book you see here. Mary Garrett, our production editor, and Hilary Powers, our copyeditor, made very valuable contributions in further shaping and improving the manuscript.

Personally, we each benefited from the support of our friends and family. Linda Katzenbach devoted considerable personal time as a critical reader of our drafts. Zia's father and mother set an (early) high bar for his research and writing. His sister Saira and her family—Ednan, Yasmeen, Nadia, and Ariana—along with friends in New York and San Francisco, provided much-needed distraction and encouragement.

About the Authors

Jon Katzenbach is a senior partner at Booz & Company and leads the Katzenbach Center at Booz, where promising new approaches in leadership, culture, and organization performance are developed for client application. His consulting career has been largely focused in these areas, and spans several decades across three different professional firms. In addition, he has written a number of articles and books, including *Wisdom of Teams, Peak Performance,* and *Why Pride Matters More Than Money.*

Katz graduated from Stanford University in 1954, where he was a member of Phi Beta Kappa, and served as a lieutenant (jg) in the U.S. Navy during the Korean War. He received his MBA from Harvard in 1959, where he was a Baker Scholar. He was also a director at McKinsey & Company and a founding partner of Katzenbach Partners.

Zia Khan is vice president for strategy and evaluation at the Rockefeller Foundation, which supports innovations that help people share globalization's benefits more equitably and strengthens their resilience to social, economic, health, and environmental challenges. Zia also advises leaders on strategy and organizational performance as a senior fellow of the Katzenbach Center, which he co-founded with Jon Katzenbach, and as an individual consultant. Prior to joining the Rockefeller Foundation, Zia was a partner at Booz & Company, which he joined after it acquired Katzenbach Partners. Zia established and led Katzenbach Partners' San Francisco office and

West Coast Practice and pioneered the firm's work on the informal organization.

Zia holds a B.S. from Cornell University and an M.S. and Ph.D. from Stanford University. He currently lives in Brooklyn, New York.

Index